Managing risk and minimising mistakes in services to children and families

Dr Lisa Bostock, Sue Bairstow, Sheila Fish and Fiona Macleod

First published in Great Britain in September 2005
by the Social Care Institute for Excellence

ISBN 1-904812-27-9

Written by Dr Lisa Bostock, Sue Bairstow, Sheila Fish and Fiona Macleod

The authors would like to thank Michael Turner, Lesley Jordan and Wendy Rose for their advice and support.

Produced by The Policy Press
Fourth Floor, Beacon House
Queen's Road
Bristol BS8 1QU
tel 0117 331 4054
fax 0117 331 4093
tpp-info@bristol.ac.uk
www.policypress.org.uk

This report is available in print and online
www.scie.org.uk

Social Care Institute for Excellence
Goldings House
2 Hay's Lane
London SE1 2HB
tel 020 7089 6840
fax 020 7089 6841
textphone 020 7089 6893
www.scie.org.uk

Acknowledgements   v

Key terms and abbreviations   vi

Summary   vii
What this report is about   vii
Getting the language right   vii
Safeguarding incidents   vii
The pilot study   vii
Policy context   viii
'No harm' incidents or near misses   ix
Complexity of needs assessment   ix
Good practice   x
Learning from safeguarding incidents   x
Involving service users and carers   xi
Suggestions for the future   xii
Conclusion   xiii

1 What the report is about   1
1.1   Introduction   1
1.2   Policy context   2
1.3   Latent and active failures   3
1.4   What this report does and doesn't do   3
1.5   Who will be interested in this report   4
1.6   Outline of report   4

2 How we did it and who took part in the study   6
2.1   Introduction   6
2.2   Project team and pilot interviews   6
2.3   The interview topic guide   7
2.4   Building trust   7
2.5   Involving service users and carers   8
2.6   Recruitment of referral and assessment   9
      social work teams
      2.6.1   Location profile   10
      2.6.2   Respondents' details: practitioners,   10
              managers and allied professionals
      2.6.3   Response rate: practitioners, managers   11
              and allied professionals
2.7   Recruitment of service users and carers   11
      2.7.1   Response rate: parents and young people   12
      2.7.2   Respondents' details: parents and   12
              young people
2.8   Learning from other sectors   13
2.9   Analysing the data   13
2.10 Conclusions   13

3   Near misses and safeguarding incidents   14
     3.1 Introduction   14
     3.2 Near misses in children's services   14
     3.3 Number of near misses identified   15
     3.4 Who identified them?   15
     3.5 Safeguarding incidents   16
     3.6 Conclusions   18

4   Risk, need and near misses   20
     4.1 Introduction   20
     4.2 Assessing need, prioritising immediate harm   20
     4.3 Near misses arising during referral and assessment   22
     4.4 Prioritising immediate harm over early intervention   24
          4.4.1 Service user and carer perspectives on   24
                 thresholds for intervention
          4.4.2 Practitioners' reflections on risk, need   25
                 and near misses
     4.5 Near misses involving problems with accessing   26
          information
     4.6 Near misses and the role of allied professionals   29
     4.7 Near misses and long-term cases   32
     4.8 Identifying underlying patterns of error   34
     4.9 Conclusion   35

5   Learning from near misses   36
     5.1 Introduction   36
     5.2 Learning organisations   36
     5.3 Cultures of blame, climates of fear and issues   37
          of leadership
     5.4 Forums for discussion, time for reflection and   41
          a reporting system
          5.4.1 Opportunities for involving service users   44
                 and carers
          5.4.2 Conclusions   45

6   Conclusion and suggestions for the future   47

     References   51

     Appendix A:Systematic search strategy   57

     Appendix B: Topic guide   64

     Appendix C: Contacting participants   67

     Appendix D: Error management and promoting   68
     patient safety – lessons from healthcare

Acknowledgements

The Social Care Institute for Excellence (SCIE) would like to thank all of the organisations and individuals who have shaped the development of this report. We gratefully acknowledge the contributions from:

- A National Voice, a user group of young people who are, or have been, looked after in England, for comments on the report and putting us in touch with other young people
- Voices from Care Cymru, a user group of young people who are, or have been, looked after in Wales, for conducting interviews with young people
- directors at the National Patient Safety Agency for taking us through their approach
- academic colleagues who have reviewed and commented on this work, particularly Dr Eileen Munro of the Social Policy Department, London School of Economics, who is the leading UK expert on using a systems approach to improving child welfare services
- Dr Andy Pithouse, School of Social Sciences, Cardiff University, and Anne Crowley, Redkite Consultancy, for their thoughtful comments and advice on the policy and practice context in Wales
- Walt Brown, SCIE research assistant, whose commitment and humour has buoyed the process and paved the way for analysis of data
- Celina Shallard for her sensitivity when interviewing parents in England
- Dr Liz Jones for her commitment when conducting interviews with social workers and allied professionals in Wales
- colleagues at SCIE, particularly those in knowledge management, for conducting the systematic search, and colleagues in practice development for providing invaluable advice.

Our greatest thanks is reserved for the social workers, managers, allied professionals and young people and parents who generously gave their time to take part in this study.

The authors would also like to thank colleagues at SCIE for their helpful comments on drafts of this report.

Key terms and abbreviations

Key terms

'Near miss': an incident where something could have gone wrong but has been prevented or did go wrong but no serious harm was caused.

'Safeguarding incident': any unintended or unexpected incident that could have or did lead to harm for social care service users and carers.

Abbreviations

ACPC	Area Child Protection Committee
ADHD	attention deficit hyperactivity disorder
ADSS	Association of Directors of Social Services
ANV	A National Voice
BME	black or minority ethnic
CAF	Common Assessment Framework
CDRG	child death review groups
CMHT	community mental health team
CSCI	Commission for Social Care Inspection
CSSR	council with social services responsibilities
DfES	Department for Education and Skills
DH	Department of Health
DHSSPS	Department of Health, Social Services and Public Safety
EDT	emergency duty team
HSE	Health and Safety Executive
IATA	International Air Transport Association
ICT	information and communications technology
LSCB	Local Safeguarding Children Board
NABSCP	National Assembly of Black Social Care Professionals
NAW	National Assembly for Wales
NHS	National Health Service
NPSA	National Patient Safety Agency
NRLS	National Reporting and Learning System
PALS	Patient Advice and Liaison Services
PSI	patient safety incident
RCA	root cause analysis
R&D	research and development
SCIE	Social Care Institute for Excellence
SSI	Social Services Inspectorate
SSIW	Social Services Inspectorate for Wales
VfCC	Voices from Care Cymru

Summary

What this report is about

This report is about how organisations can learn from mistakes. In the past, learning has tended to take place when things have gone seriously wrong for children, when they have been hurt or, worse, killed.

The report discusses an organisational focus on learning, best described as 'learning from experience' in the inquiry into the death of Victoria Climbié. It aims to shift the focus and start a debate about the management of risk at an organisational level, as distinct from the assessment of need for an individual child.

The report demonstrates that there are ways to learn from potentially adverse events before harm is caused to children and their families. This paper aims to support the introduction of the Children Act 2004 in England and Wales, including the development of Local Safeguarding Children Boards (LSCBs).

Getting the language right

Drawing on developments in other sectors, including healthcare, this approach is known as 'risk management' and refers to organisational processes that promote learning from mistakes as a means to improve safety for service users and carers.

Safeguarding incidents

The report therefore introduces a new language for describing adverse events and near misses – when things almost go wrong within children's services. It develops the idea of 'safeguarding incidents'. Safeguarding incidents cover everything that could have or did cause harm to children and families. It focuses specifically on 'no harm' incidents or near misses. This is because research shows that learning from 'free mistakes' such as these can prevent more serious incidents in the future.

The safeguarding incidents described in the report are based on actual practice examples. Again, we tend to understand such incidents at the level of individual practice of a child's assessment of need. The report aims to understand these examples differently and use them to examine how organisations can learn from and build on experience.

The pilot study

The report is based on a pilot study of organisational approaches to risk management, including opportunities for learning from safeguarding incidents. It draws on the following:

- an overview of literature on learning from mistakes in health and social care
- interviews with more than 60 social workers and their managers and allied professionals across eight local authorities in England and Wales
- ethnographic work with three referral and assessment teams, two in England and one in Wales

- group interviews with just under 40 young people in care and with families in contact with social services, about their experiences of things that could go wrong and how these should be managed.

> On this mistake management thing, there's a culture of shame around mistakes and that needs to be addressed at its core. My teacher used to say: 'Everyone makes mistakes – that's why they put rubbers on the end of pencils!' We need to encourage an open culture about mistakes so that we really can learn from them.
>
> *Young person*

Policy context

Risk management programmes that promote learning from adverse events and near misses have proved to be a powerful means of improving safety. This approach has been pioneered within aviation and, more recently, adopted by the healthcare sector within the UK.

In July 2001, the government set up the National Patient Safety Agency (NPSA) to coordinate the efforts to learn from adverse incidents and near misses occurring in the National Health Service (NHS) in England and Wales. The NPSA uses root cause analysis (RCA) techniques to understand the underlying causes of incidents rather than identifying individual failure.

> There are courses on patient safety that are run by people who are in the aviation industry. And they will tell you that – I've been on one – that most disasters are caused by the result of a sequence of smaller events, and I think the same probably applies in social work as other areas of the health service.
>
> *Parent*

The introduction of LSCBs will replace Area Child Protection Committees (ACPCs), which currently commission serious case reviews. LSCBs will set up child death review groups (CDRGs). These will review information on the deaths of *all* children in the local authority area – not just those in contact with organisations charged with safeguarding their welfare – and draw conclusions on what can be learned to prevent or reduce the numbers of deaths from whatever causes in the future.

The development of CDRGs represents an opportunity to apply RCA techniques to serious case reviews. This should lead to a 'systems approach' to the analysis of adverse incidents, one that takes human error as the starting point and not the conclusion of the investigation, by looking at *why* mistakes are made rather than by *whom*.

> I felt a personal as well as professional responsibility to get it right. This all contributes to anxiety. The reality is, if you make a wrong decision lots of people, particularly children, will suffer.
>
> *Social worker*

'No harm' incidents or near misses

A focus on safeguarding incidents introduces the possibility of LSCBs reviewing 'no harm' incidents, or 'near misses', as well as serious cases and child deaths.

Near misses consist of the following:

* something could have gone wrong but has been prevented
* something did go wrong but no serious harm was caused.

Using the above definition, 60 near misses were identified by respondents. They were more likely to be identified by frontline staff, who described two thirds of all examples. Where senior managers identified near misses, almost all had been raised by external agencies, usually in the form of complaints.

Respondents also reported 15 serious safeguarding incidents, involving serious injury or the death of child, where local agencies suspect abuse or neglect is involved.

This report presents case studies of near misses identified by social workers and their managers. Their descriptions of near misses cluster around the following themes:

* The everyday nature of near misses makes them hard to identify.
* The risk of harm to children can be missed during referral and assessment.
* Complacency on long-term cases can allow a risk of harm to go unnoticed.

Complexity of needs assessment

Assessing the needs of children, including the need to safeguard them from significant harm, is complex. This means that many near misses involve cases where actual or potential significant harm to children has been overlooked. In other cases, workers may misjudge a family as a false risk to their children.

The predominance of a focus on risk of immediate harm to children rather than assessment of need and early intervention is also apparent in the case examples. In other words, the needs of children had been overlooked or resources were not available until risk of immediate harm was apparent. Parents in the current study confirm this.

Many near misses during the referral and assessment stage arise due to:

* the prioritisation of cases
* professionals not having an accurate or full picture of what is happening
* decisions made by other teams and agencies.

> In my situation, because he's not an abused child – I'm not hitting him or I'm not an alcoholic, I'm not a drug addict – he's not a priority. But that doesn't help me. I mean, there's all kind of abuse. I mean, at the moment, he's abusing himself. At the end of the day, he is still a child in need.
>
> *Parent*

It should be noted that this report focuses primarily on active failures – those that are made by frontline staff – at the expense of exploring latent failures that are embedded in the system and create the conditions for active failure. Latent failures are associated with the actions and decisions of those not in the frontline, such as politicians and policy-makers, senior management and designers.

This emphasis on active failures is a reflection of our focus on frontline staff, service users and carers rather than on senior managers. Any future study needs to include the latter as major players in the total scenario. Making the system safer may require change at any level, not just those close to service-user contact.

Good practice

Most of the near misses identified refer to situations where something could have gone wrong but was prevented rather than cases where something had gone wrong and no harm was caused.

The NPSA call this the 'phew factor' ('Phew! That didn't go wrong but what about next time?'). These incidents, while containing a sense of relief that nothing harmful has happened, also allow workers to feel good about their practice because they have actively intervened to prevent something from going wrong. This was reflected in many of the examples described by respondents in the current study, where good practice, safe decision-making and robust safeguarding are all apparent.

Learning from safeguarding incidents

Systems for safeguarding children that acknowledge the complexity of assessment and promote learning rather than blame are better able – as a means to improve services – to promote discussion of safeguarding incidents where harm or potential harm is missed or misdiagnosed.

Currently, there are few opportunities for organisations to learn from near misses. Where learning occurs, it is located at the frontline, in supervision between social workers and their managers. In fact, respondents reported concern that learning from serious case reviews was still limited.

One step towards learning from safeguarding incidents is the establishing of a reporting system. The development of the National Reporting and Learning System (NRLS) based at the NPSA means that health professionals are actively encouraged to report adverse incidents and near misses to improve patient safety.

> We don't have a reporting system, although I do increasingly think that should be the case. People should be encouraged rather than discouraged, rather than just covering their back, people should be saying: 'We've got a problem here and we want somebody to unpack it with us and look at it.'
>
> *Service manager*

Learning from safeguarding incidents is dependent on five fundamental features of a learning organisation:

* structure
* organisational culture
* information systems
* human resources practices
* leadership.

This means that work to promote learning from safeguarding incidents can take place in different aspects of an organisation – by a commitment from leaders to understand the underlying causes of incidents as well as by the growth of robust human resource systems to help develop practice.

Involving service users and carers

Harnessing the knowledge and expertise of service users and carers presents a key means for learning about safeguarding incidents and improving systems to protect and promote the welfare of children.

LSCBs represent a good opportunity for organisational learning to take place across agencies. There may also be benefits in exploring their potential to look at all safeguarding incidents, including near misses.

Given the number and diversity of near misses identified in the current study, service-user and carer representatives on LSCBs may help prioritise which cases need to be analysed thoroughly to improve practice.

> I can't undo my disaster now. It happened. I'm in it. But if we can stop the same thing happening to a few other people, then I'm happy to help.
>
> *Parent*

Young people and parents also welcome an open discussion about mistakes. This means apologising for them, involving children and families in any subsequent analysis of their cause(s) and showing commitment to learning from safeguarding incidents to improve practice.

This would serve to restore trust in social services and help families begin to recover from what are often painful experiences.

> We don't know what mistakes they [social workers] make because they never let on. They should be encouraged to own up, *apologise*, and as long as they improve, then they should be allowed to stay on.
>
> *Young person*

Suggestions for the future

This report makes the following suggestions for the future:

Policy

1. Explore options for a parallel to NPSA in social care to promote an open and fair culture, encouraging all staff and other stakeholders such as politicians and policy-makers to understand their role in decision-making and preventing error.
2. Consider whether the development and implementation of LSCBs alongside other systems could include a focus on the range of safeguarding incidents rather than one that is solely directed on unexpected child deaths or the serious injury of children.
3. Increase capacity within local authorities to adopt a systems approach, introduce critical reporting systems/forums and root cause analysis techniques for understanding why things do, or almost, go wrong.

Research

4. Survey developments towards the creation of a culture of learning within local authority and voluntary agencies charged with safeguarding children, focusing on efforts to tackle the blame culture, on forums for reflection and on how well frontline workers are supported in their efforts to create safety.
5. Explore latent failures embedded within organisations as well as active failures made by frontline staff, going beyond surface error to identify underlying patterns in order to devise solutions.

Practice development

6. Pilot the introduction of critical incident reporting within children's services, exploring how best to promote an open and blame-free approach to learning from safeguarding incidents as a prerequisite to the development of such a system.
7. Develop a professional network for referral and assessment workers to promote good practice in complex decision-making.

These suggestions present the first steps towards developing a systems approach to risk management within children's services that allows for complexity and encourages learning from frontline practice, including critical events.

> It's a very interesting way to approach it, isn't it? I'm used to taking this kind of approach from a health and safety perspective – 'Oh look, someone's tripped over the mat, it's a near miss, we need to make sure we do something about that' – but I'm not used to using that as a way of focusing on children's safety. I think it's quite a useful thing to do, and perhaps we need to build it in a bit better to the way that we think about it.
>
> *Voluntary sector worker*

Conclusion

This report argues that we will be better able to learn how to protect children and young people if we look at so-called near misses as well as at incidents of serious harm.

Adding this perspective would allow child safeguarding systems to be developed in the light of an understanding that mistakes are integral to human services, and that the objective is to learn how to catch mistakes at an early enough stage to prevent serious consequences.

In some industries, this approach is termed *safety management*: by identifying adverse incidents and near misses and establishing systems that monitor and correct them, it has produced a tangible reduction in harm to people who use the services.

In child welfare, we propose the term *safeguarding incident* to capture near misses as well as incidents causing serious harm. Analyses of near misses reveal weaknesses in the necessarily complex assessment, decision-making and review systems surrounding child welfare and show ways of correcting them. This suggests that children and families who use social services will – just like patients and rail and air passengers – benefit from the application of safety management.

1 What the report is about

1.1 Introduction

This report examines organisational approaches to learning from mistakes. It presents the position put forward by the Social Care Institute for Excellence (SCIE) on new ways for organisations charged with the responsibility of safeguarding children to understand and learn from adverse incidents to improve the safety and quality of services to children and families. The report into the death of Victoria Climbié describes this type of organisational learning as 'learning from experience'.[1]

> A healthy culture begins with high-quality leadership by senior managers willing to 'walk the talk' and who are anxious to understand the issues facing frontline staff. It grows once people are willing to analyse their individual practice and contemplate change. That in turn requires management being willing to adopt, not a blame-free culture, but a learning culture. Individual responsibility had to be recognised, but there needed to be a willingness to accept that it was possible for teams and individuals to fail, to learn from their mistakes, and to start again.
>
> *Victoria Climbié Inquiry*[1]

One way to identify areas for improvement in service provision is through learning from 'no harm' incidents or 'near misses'. Near misses are incidents where harm could have occurred but has been prevented, or incidents that have occurred but no harm was caused. In the health sector, learning from 'free mistakes' such as these has been shown to reduce future risk of adverse events and improve the safety of patients.[2] In social care provision, children's services have yet to adopt this approach.

There is increasing recognition within the social work research community that social care should embrace similar approaches to risk management now adopted by healthcare, including dealing with near misses.[3-9] Yet, to date, the feasibility of such a move has not been investigated; the very nature of near misses in childcare social work has not been researched.

Consequently, this report focuses specifically on the feasibility of reducing risk by identifying and learning from near misses in children's services. It presents the findings of a unique piece of research conducted with social work staff, parents and young people. Please note that the area of social work practice that is the focus of this study is called 'services to children and families'. However, the status of parents in this area remains ambiguous, making the term 'service users and carers' problematic. Are parents best understood as carers of their service-user children or as themselves service users? Addressing this dilemma is beyond the confines of this report. Consequently, we use the 'service users and carers' to refer to children, their parents and other significant adults while acknowledging the limitations of doing so.

The report presents evidence of the kinds of near misses that currently occur, the contexts in which they happen and explanations given of their causes. It details mechanisms for and inhibitors to learning from these incidents. From these data, it draws out implications for policy and practice development towards improving the quality of children's services and the safety of children. The report aims to support the introduction of the Children Act 2004 in England and Wales, and to feed into developments in Northern Ireland concerning the improvement of the safety of patients and service users, led by the Department of Health, Social Services and Public Safety (DHSSPS).

To this end, the report introduces the concept of the 'safeguarding incident' to capture the range of things that do, or almost, go wrong in children's services. 'Safeguarding incident' is a new term for describing adverse incidents within children's services and, more broadly, within social care. Safeguarding incidents are graded to capture the range of seriousness from 'no harm' incidents through to child death. A focus on safeguarding incidents rather than solely on severe or serious cases promotes the possibility of learning from potentially adverse events before harm is caused to service users and carers.

1.2 Policy context

In July 2001, the government set up the National Patient Safety Agency (NPSA) to coordinate nationally efforts to learn from adverse incidents and near misses that affect patient safety in the NHS. This followed the recommendations made in *An organisation with a memory*,[10] which highlighted both the scale of avoidable events in the NHS that result in harm to patients and the lack of systematic learning from them. The report was highly critical of the 'culture of blame' prevalent in the NHS, which focuses attention only on the actions of the individuals involved in an incident. Instead, it recommended a 'systems approach' to identifying and redressing the causes of mistakes.

> Patient safety has been an under-recognised and under-researched concept ... the recognition that human error is inevitable in a highly complex and technical field like medicine is a first step in promoting greater awareness of the importance of systems failure in the causation of accidents.
> *Liam Donaldson, Chief Medical Officer, Department of Health*[11]

The NPSA is introducing the National Reporting and Learning System (NRLS) to facilitate the identification of clusters of similar adverse incidents at a national level. It is also promoting a new way of analysing them. Traditionally, analysis has focused on identifying individual failure. Using root cause analysis (RCA), the NPSA is encouraging attention to failures in the systems within which people work in order to understand the underlying causes of adverse incidents. They advocate the importance of involving service users and carers in the process of identification and analysis. Moreover, the NPSA is promoting an open and fair culture in which healthcare staff report incidents without undue fear of personal reprimand. Without this, neither reporting nor learning from such incidents is likely to take place. (For more information, including details of RCA training and toolkit, please visit the NPSA website: www.npsa.nhs.uk/.)

In *Keep children safe*,[12] its response to the findings of the Laming Report into the death of Victoria Climbié,[1] the government proposes a new system for examining unexpected child deaths in England, which draws on the expertise of the NPSA. It recommends that the current serious case review system for reviewing such incidents would benefit from more of a 'systems approach' to examining why these incidents happen and what can be done to reduce the likelihood of further ones. The Welsh Assembly Government also made an extensive response to the Climbié Inquiry (for more information, please visit www.wales.gov.uk/subichildren/content/responses/resp_climbie-e.htm).

> We are expecting Local Safeguarding Children Boards to establish local screening teams to learn lessons and apply those lessons at a local level.
> *Althea Efunshile, Director of Safeguarding Children and*
> *Supporting Families, Department for Education and Skills*[13]

Following the introduction of the Children Act 2004, Local Safeguarding Children Boards (LSCBs) will replace Area Child Protection Committees (ACPCs). LSCBs will set up child death review groups (CDRGs), which will consist of a range of appointed professionals to examine all unexpected child deaths.[14] As identified in *Keep children safe*, the use of RCA techniques could lead to a 'systems approach' to the analysis, which takes human error as the starting point for the investigation and not its conclusion, by looking at *why* mistakes are made rather than *by whom*. It may also be worth exploring the possibility of extending the role of LSCBs to include reviewing all safeguarding incidents as well as unexpected child death as this represents an opportunity to look at organisational learning before harm is caused to children.

1.3 Latent and active failures

A systems perspective on organisational failure (errors and accidents) has been developed by the psychologist James Reason.[15-18] He has introduced the related concepts of 'active failures' and 'latent failures' to express the multi-level nature of accident causation. Reason argues that the effects of active failures or errors are felt almost immediately and are associated with the actions of frontline workers – i.e. errors of judgement and lapses in performance. Latent failures, however, are found deeper in the system and only become visible when they combine with other factors to create error. They are more often due to the actions of people not in frontline work: policy-makers, senior managers and designers.

It should be remembered that active failures are neither necessary nor sufficient in and of themselves to cause an accident. To help explain this, Reason uses Swiss cheese as an analogy (*see* Figure 1). Slices of cheese that is full of holes represent an organisation's layers of defence against error. The holes in defence mechanisms due to latent and active failures are always changing. When the holes in defences due to latent conditions and active failures line up, accidents will occur – e.g. a child is severely injured while an assessment is underway.[9,15]

1.4 What this report does and doesn't do

This report identifies 'active failures' well but is less effective in identifying latent ones. This is because the pilot study collected data primarily from frontline workers, parents and young people. Any future study would need to identify latent as well as active failures, looking beyond surface error to explore the underlying patterns to devise solutions. By focusing on active failure at the expense of understanding underlying causes, we are in danger of echoing the bias of traditional inquiries, which saw improvement being achieved primarily by changes in the performance of frontline workers and low-level managers.

Figure 1: Reason's Swiss cheese model[17]

Nevertheless, the key strengths of the study are its findings that the systems approach can be meaningfully applied in the field of child welfare, that frontline workers and their seniors are willing to cooperate and to be open about their mistakes, and that families can also be engaged and provide valuable insights into the work.[19]

1.5 Who will be interested in this report

The report is aimed at those who are seeking to promote a better understanding of why things go wrong, in order to improve systems for the management of risk, including the analysis of safeguarding incidents. The report will be useful to the following groups:

* members of Area Child Protection Committees (ACPCs) and, in the future, LSCBs
* senior managers within statutory and voluntary childcare agencies
* quality assurance managers
* frontline practitioners and their managers
* post-qualifying social work consortia
* social work researchers and educators
* social care inspectors in England, Wales and Northern Ireland
* service users and carers
* allied professionals involved in child protection and supporting families
* Association of Directors of Social Services (ADSS).

1.6 Outline of report

Following this introduction, the report continues by detailing how the study into near misses in children's services was carried out. Chapter 2 begins by highlighting the ground-breaking nature of this research, describing the difficulties inherent in conducting research into such a sensitive issue and the steps that were taken to make it feasible. It explains how the study was carried out and profiles its participants.

With Chapter 3, the presentation of the findings of our study begins. Simple statistical data is presented to demonstrate how many near misses respondents identified and who identified them. To open the possibility of capturing such 'free mistakes' in risk management strategies, the new language of 'safeguarding incidents' is then introduced.

Drawing on the kinds of examples of near misses that respondents gave, as well as their commentary about them, Chapter 4 builds a more complex picture of near misses. Findings are presented about the general context within which near misses frequently take place and factors significant to why they happen. Practitioners, parents and young people emerge as valuable sources of knowledge about these safeguarding incidents. Similarities and differences in their opinions about why near misses happen are explored.

Chapter 5 addresses the question of whether opportunities currently exist to learn from experiences of near misses, both individually and organisationally. Drawing on a framework of 'learning organisations', we detail opportunities and barriers to such learning that respondents in the study identified. We highlight significant findings about the feasibility of including service users and carers in the identification and analysis of safeguarding incidents more generally. The benefits that such involvement would bring are clarified.

Implications for policy and practice development are drawn out in the conclusion that forms Chapter 6. In addition, suggestions are made for further research that would build on the findings of this report.

2. How we did it and who took part in the study

2.1 Introduction

This study represents the first attempt to collect data about near misses in children's services. At the beginning of the study, we had no evidence that near misses actually featured in childcare social work, nor that social workers or service users would relate to the concept. We had little information of which social work teams would be the best source of knowledge about them. Furthermore, we were also aware that social workers and their managers might be extremely reluctant to take part in the study.

Inquiry reports into the deaths of children known to statutory services tend to identify specific individuals as responsible and highlight their particular failings, with little consideration for the context within which they work.[4,6] Inquiry reports invariably attract intense media attention as well. This has created a fear of getting it wrong or of the consequences of being seen to get it wrong.[20] It has led some authors to comment on a tendency towards defensive or risk averse practice in children's services.[21-25] One consequence of defensive practice is a reluctance to discuss mistakes, because mistakes are viewed as 'getting it wrong' rather than integral to the human condition within which 'to err is human'.

This chapter addresses these issues and looks at how we set up and conducted the study. It clarifies the questions we wanted to investigate, describes who took part and the research methods we used. The report is also underpinned by a systematic search of the literature. Not all literature included from the search has been used in the report, which largely focuses on research exploring risk management in children's services. Further analysis should be conducted on the literature examining error management in other sectors (*see* Appendix A). In this chapter, we focus on the primary, qualitative research.

2.2 Project team and pilot interviews

Venturing into such uncharted territory in research and development (R&D) work, we decided that a staged approach to the project was appropriate. First, we ensured that the research team included social workers as well as researchers to reflect its R&D remit. Second, pilot interviews were conducted with nine respondents to help shape the project. These individuals – who all worked within referral and assessment teams and quality assurance departments – were identified via contacts of the project team.

The pilot interviews aimed to help us develop methods for talking to social workers about their experience of adverse incidents generally and near misses in particular. They helped us begin to refine our definition of near misses as they feature in children's services. We also wanted to 'test the water' and get an indication of how practitioners felt about the rationale of our project. We explained the 'systems approach' and the focus on organisational learning as opposed to individual blame. We asked people how they felt about a research project that aimed to look at learning from mistakes in this way. We requested their advice on the most suitable approach.

In total, nine respondents from six local authorities were interviewed in this way. One respondent who was a service manager conducted her own group interview with five members of a referral and assessment team and their manager about their understandings of and explanations for near misses. Where data is drawn from the group interview, it will be identified as 'Group interview, referral and assessment team', rather than referring to the professional position of the respondent. These pilot interviews informed in a number of ways how we set up and planned the research.

2.3 The interview topic guide

On the basis of the pilot interviews, we refined our understanding of what constituted a near miss. At the beginning of the research, we used the terms 'close calls' and 'near misses' interchangeably. This was because we were testing the language and were unclear about which phrase would best describe such incidents. It also means that respondents sometimes refer to 'close calls' rather than 'near misses' in the extracts.

It became increasingly clear that the term 'near miss' captured more accurately the nature of potentially adverse incidents. And, crucially, through the pilot interviews it also became apparent that near misses really did feature regularly in children's services.

The pilot interviews also shaped the themes and questions we prepared for conducting interviews. It had become apparent that it was difficult to talk about near misses without also talking about risk assessment and decision-making. Given that more than one person would be conducting interviews, a topic guide was developed to guide conversations with respondents (*see* Appendix B). The topic guide covered two general themes:

- understanding risk, thresholds and decision-making
- learning from near misses.

2.4 Building trust

Conducting pilot interviews on the issue of near misses heightened our awareness of the importance of building trust with the social work teams. Across the respondent sample, responses ranged from reticent to resentful at the prospect of yet more attention on what social workers do wrong, overlooking all their good practice.

> It's just so negative, it's knee-jerk, stop focusing on the negative. Go and look at what work I have done to minimise this ultimate risk – of all the good decisions I made to keep a family from dissolving.
>
> *Student social worker*

> If people are talking about near misses, it's like with any research – it depends on what the actual aim is gonna be, how it's gonna be used. It could be about blaming social workers again. I haven't got much trust in things like that …
>
> *Social worker*

We decided, therefore, that one-off interviews were not appropriate for this research. Instead, we planned to incorporate an ethnographic research method into our study by spending three weeks with each team, over a period of three months. The research method was 'ethnographic' because it involved entering someone else's world in order to understand their perspectives – i.e. by going out and talking to them wherever they were and whatever they were doing. We hoped that this approach would allow a higher level of trust between researchers and respondents than a one-off encounter.

Input from the pilot interviews had underlined the need for absolute clarity about the focus and the purpose of our research. Our focus on systems as opposed to individuals, and on learning as opposed to blaming, therefore, needed to be reflected in our research methods. All respondents were offered confidentiality, unless a child was at risk. In the event, no need to use the child protection protocol arose during the course of the research. We also made it clear that the respondents' anonymity would be preserved. As a result, in this report individual respondents are not identified by their location, respondent number, gender or ethnic background.

Further to these measures, we also requested access to decision-making forums, such as strategy meetings and child protection conferences, as well as conducting interviews. The aim was to allow us to observe decision-making in practice. We hoped both to gain and to be seen to gain a more 'organic' understanding of the realities of childcare social work practice than a focus on individuals out of context would ever allow. By this means, we hoped to reinforce our verbal explanations that the aim of this study was not to give social workers another 'knuckle rapping'.

To demonstrate our interest in the potential of a systems approach to learning from near misses, in which practitioners feature as sources of knowledge, a broadly participative approach was necessary. The issue of trust raised through the pilot interviews strengthened our resolution to conduct further interviews in such a way that respondents were encouraged to take the lead on the issues that they considered crucial to the subject of near misses. No time limits were placed on the interviews. On average, they lasted one hour, and in a small number of cases, they continued on a subsequent day.

We also involved participants in later stages of the project. From the beginning, respondents were informed of a 'feedback' session to which they would be invited. By this means, we aimed to give them the opportunity to meet other teams who had taken part in the study, to hear and comment on our findings and what we were doing with the work. This session was so successful that further feedback sessions have since taken place.

All localities were also offered training on SCIE's free resource, the electronic Library for Social Care, now called Social Care Online. For more information, please visit www.scie-socialcareonline.org.uk.

2.5 Involving service users and carers

Service users and carers represent a key source of knowledge about the services of which they partake. This study aimed to incorporate the expertise of young people and parents with experience of children's services on why mistakes happen and the potential for learning from them, as well as opportunities and obstacles to that process. As a result, in addition to engaging with social work teams and allied professionals, interviews with service users were planned.

Another emerging theme from the pilot interviews concerned the routine nature of near misses. There was some suggestion that near misses happen all the time. The question arose, therefore, as to whether some near misses provide better learning opportunities than others. We decided that an important element of our study was to find out which near misses young people and parents considered to be a priority for learning.

2.6 Recruitment of referral and assessment social work teams

Having planned our research methods in this way, the next phase of the project involved identifying and recruiting social work teams to take part in the study. The decision was made to base the study on referral and assessment teams. These are the first port of access to children's services, taking all referrals from the public as well as from professionals and conducting assessments of children's needs.

> [The referral and assessment team] is the social services department's frontline. If the work is not identified, diagnosed and actioned appropriately, the situation of children referred for help may become unsafe. All referrals, new and previously known, come first to the referral and assessment team: hence, an immediate diagnosis is required to identify the nature of the problem. Decisions are needed at the very first contact point about the degree of urgency, the degree of risk and the degree of need.[26]

Decisions made by social workers during this initial contact determine how cases are subsequently responded to. In some cases, failure to revise initial judgements in the light of new evidence can lead to tragic consequences and has featured in many inquiry reports.[27] Most recently, the decision to define Victoria Climbié as 'a child in need' rather than as 'a child in need of protection' meant that the risk posed to her was overlooked in favour of more benign explanations.[1] We surmised, therefore, that near misses were likely to be experienced by these teams. Basing the study on these teams, however, would not prevent us from involving senior managers, including quality assurance managers and service managers, who all have an explicit role to play in terms of practice development and improving the quality of the service.

Two teams were recruited from England, where fieldwork was conducted from May to August 2004. Following a request in July 2004 from the Welsh Assembly, a third referral and assessment team was recruited in Wales. This team was included so that the study could contribute to the *Safeguarding Vulnerable Children Review* (for more information, please visit www.wales.gov.uk/subichildren/content/svcr-invite-evidence-e.htm). Fieldwork was conducted by the team in Wales from October to December 2004 and included interviews with allied professionals, including representatives from the police, paediatrics, education and the voluntary sector (*see below*). (*See also* Appendix C for a discussion of how the three teams were recruited into the study.)

2.6.1 Location profile

Location A is a London borough with deprivation levels among the highest in the country. Over a quarter of the people in Location A are black or from a minority ethnic group.

Location B is one of the largest counties in England. There are above average levels of deprivation, ill health and long-term disability in some urban areas. As a county, it is ethnically diverse.

Location C consists of a mix of small towns and valley communities. It has a high rate of poverty, and its population is overwhelmingly white.

Including all the authorities that took part in the initial pilot interviews, performance ratings of the eight English local authorities in the current study ranged from 1* to 3*. The ratings refer to the performance of 'councils with social services responsibilities' (CSSRs) measured against a set of predefined criteria. The Commission for Social Care Inspection (CSCI) assesses councils in order to produce the ratings[28] (for more information, please visit www.csci.org.uk/council_performance/star_ratings/default.htm). The Social Services Inspectorate for Wales (SSIW) does not operate this system (please visit www.wales.gov.uk/subisocialpolicysocialservices for more information).

2.6.2 Respondents' details: practitioners, managers and allied professionals

Table 1 identifies the number of respondents by locality. Differences reflect the varying sizes of the teams, with the team based within Location B being smaller than those based in Locations A and C.

Table 1: Number of respondents

Location	Respondents
Pilots	14
Location A	19
Location B	09
Location C	20
Total	**62**

Table 2 indicates the status of respondents within their organisations. The majority of them were frontline social workers, senior practitioners, specialist workers and their managers. Specialist workers have specific practice development roles within referral and assessment teams, such as African workers and health visitors. There are also senior managers who all have an explicit role to play in terms of practice development and improving the quality of the service to children and families. At the request of the Welsh Assembly, a small number of allied professionals were interviewed in Wales. They have a crucial role to play in safeguarding children, and future research in this area should pay more attention to their perspectives.

Table 2: Status within organisation

Status	Number
Referral and information officers	02
Family support workers	02
Student social workers	02
Social workers	16
Senior practitioners	03
Specialist workers	02
Team leaders	04
Frontline managers	07
Service managers	03
Quality assurance managers	04
Senior managers	07
Allied professionals	05
Total	**57**

Please note that data in Table 2 exclude those who took part in the group interview because we do not know the status, gender or ethnic identity of any of those individuals.

The majority of the sample were women (42/57), 15 respondents were men. Respondents from a white European, South African or Australasian background made up the majority of the sample (52/57); five respondents were from a black or minority ethnic (BME) group.

2.6.3 Response rate: practitioners, managers and allied professionals

The overall response ratewas 82 per cent, but differed by locality. Location C reported the highest response rate at 100 per cent, Location B reported 90 per cent but Location A reported only 68 per cent. Some people did not step forward to be interviewed when asked, others cancelled interviews and were unable to rearrange them and one person cited fear of 'saying the wrong thing' for their refusal.

Fewer respondents from BME groups were interviewed than anticipated. This may reflect a reluctance to take part in a study being conducted by white researchers for a largely white organisation such as SCIE. More subtly, in light of the Laming Report there may be a sense among BME social workers that they have been singled out as responsible for failings within children's services, and hence a topic about identifying and learning from mistakes may have been even more off-putting.[29,30] This issue has also been raised by the National Assembly of Black Social Care Professionals (NABSCP), one of whose objectives is to improve the public perception of black practitioners in the aftermath of the deaths of Victoria Climbié and Toni-Ann Byfield (more information about NABSCP can be accessed at www.basw.co.uk).

2.7 Recruitment of service users and carers

In England, service users and carers were recruited from locations different to the local authority where the pilot study was taking place. Considering that social workers are so used to being blamed, we felt that they would be more reluctant to take part if we were seeking views from service users that they had actually assessed. In view of the positive experience in England, on negotiating access to the Welsh local authority we requested that we be introduced to local service user and carer forums.

Young people in England were contacted via a care leavers group in London. We were introduced to this group by the London development worker for A National Voice (ANV), a service-user organisation of young people who are or have been in care. Parents were contacted via a family group meetings (FGMs) project in the north-west of England. FGMs are family-led decision-making forums that address the question of how best to provide for children's needs.

In Wales, young people were contacted via a local leaving care group, and parents were contacted via a support group for parents. Voices from Care Cymru (VfCC), a service-user organisation of young people who are or have been in care, also conducted five interviews with young people.

All respondents were interviewed in a group setting. Parents in England were also asked to take part in in-depth individual interviews.

2.7.1 Response rate: parents and young people

Some young people expressed reluctance to take part in the study, citing 'consultation fatigue' and the experience of having received no feedback on previous contributions. Parents were more ready to take part, which may reflect their more ambiguous position as service users within a framework where children's needs come first. Nevertheless, a 100 per cent response rate was reported across the groups of both young people and parents.

All were paid for their time, either in cash or in the form of a voucher.[31] Feedback sessions have also taken place.

2.7.2 Respondents' details: parents and young people

All the young people involved in this study had experience of care, while parents had all experienced the initial assessment process. Table 3 shows that, of the 25 children and young people in care (or who had recently left care) who were interviewed, 18 were girls/young women, compared with seven boys/young men. Nineteen of the young people were white, while six of them identified themselves as belonging to a BME group.

The number of parents interviewed totalled 13, all of whom were white. All but one were female (12/13).

Table 3: Numbers of young people and parents (England and Wales)

	England	Wales
Young people	10	15
Parents	06	07

2.8 Learning from other sectors

Tape-recorded interviews were also conducted with three directors of the National Patient Safety Agency (*see* Appendix D for a discussion of the role of the NPSA and how they promote learning from patient safety incidents). These interviews covered the role of the NPSA, methods for identifying and analysing adverse events and near misses, and suggestions for learning points for social care.

2.9 Analysing the data

Data were analysed using themes. Data were loaded into the qualitative data analysis package Atlas.ti and a set of *a priori* codes applied, which focused on definitions of risk, thresholds, decision-making, examples of close calls and near misses, and learning mechanisms. Atlas.ti was primarily used as a data management package that enabled the research team to access information quickly.

Detailed analysis of these data took place by hand and through team discussions about emerging themes. Divergent as well as convergent themes were noted. Some divergent themes from respondents in the sample of practitioners, for example, depended on their location. What was perhaps more surprising was the convergence of responses, given the diversity of the sample.

For instance, it was clear that, when respondents were describing opportunities to learn from mistakes, much of what they discussed was aspirational rather than current practice. Only one team had instigated practice development meetings, which respondents hoped would be a forum to explore near misses (but had not yet tested this). On the other hand, data on barriers to learning was focused almost exclusively on the difficulties of working and *learning* within a blame culture that was fuelled by the fear of child fatality, particularly in families known to the child welfare system.

2.10 Conclusions

This report is based on a complex data set, drawing on a relatively large number of respondents (100) for a small-scale qualitative research project. The data were analysed so as to build a picture of near misses in children's services, the contexts within which they occur and how we might best learn from them and so prevent unnecessary harm to children. This picture is presented over the next three chapters.

The honesty of all those who took part in identifying adverse incidents and near misses, despite concern that findings would be used negatively, is testimony to their commitment to improving individual and organisational practice for service users.

3 Near misses and safeguarding incidents

3.1 Introduction

This chapter presents unique examples from the study of near misses that have occurred in children's services. It presents details of the numbers of near misses described by respondents and the people most likely to identify them. In this way, the chapter presents an unprecedented insight into the importance of paying attention to near misses for risk management strategies.

In this light, the chapter opens up discussion about the significance of grading adverse incidents within children's services to include a range of outcomes, including instances where no harm was caused. It adapts concepts developed by the National Patient Safety Agency (NPSA) about adverse incidents and near misses in healthcare to develop a new language for describing adverse incidents and near misses in social care, specifically in children's services.

3.2 Near misses in children's services

In children's services, adverse incidents that are identified tend to be at the very serious end of the spectrum. These are known as 'serious cases' and involve the unlawful killing of or serious injury to children in circumstances giving rise to concern. Such cases are reviewed by Area Child Protection Committees (ACPCs) under government guidance outlined in *Working together to safeguard children*.[32] As we have already stated, 'no harm' incidents or near misses do not feature in social work research. Therefore, we begin this chapter very simply with three examples from our study.

> Case: Concerns had been expressed about the baby carried by a pregnant woman with mental health problems. The woman went missing before a pre-birth assessment had been completed. The hospital was alerted, but the child protection system responsible for picking it up failed and social services were not notified. By chance, a nurse saw a 'missing person' note on the hospital noticeboard, made the link and informed social services. The whereabouts of the woman was uncovered and no serious harm had been caused.
>
> *Group interview, referral and assessment team*

> Case: There was a referral concerning potential neglect of children by a mother with mental health problems and offending behaviour. The mother refused entry to her home and would hold the children up to the window and shout: 'There's one, there's the other one, they're fine, bugger off!' The probation worker viewed the mother as her primary responsibility rather than the child, and the mental health team would not intervene because the mother had not requested help. Subsequently, the mother was sectioned and the children placed with the grandparents. No serious harm was caused. The children were, however, left in a neglectful situation longer than perhaps necessary.
>
> *Social worker*

> Case: A newborn baby of a mother with learning disabilities was referred to children's services because of the need to support mother and baby. The extent of

the mother's need for extra support and the risk to her child if that support was not provided had not been picked up at antenatal stage or in hospital. Within a matter of hours of leaving hospital, the mother had shaken the baby who, luckily, was unhurt. The baby has since been placed for adoption.

Group interview, referral and assessment team

Respondents had little problem relating to the concept of near misses, nor in identifying them from their own experience. In the face of such a scarcity of documentation about near misses in children's social work, we have counted the numbers of examples they gave. We recognise the sound critiques of counting within qualitative research but have found it useful to build up a picture of whether near misses are commonly identified and by whom.

> ... simple counting techniques can offer a means to survey the whole corpus [body] of data ordinarily lost in intensive, qualitative research. Instead of taking the researcher's word for it, the reader has a chance to gain a sense of the flavour of the data as a whole. In turn, researchers are able to test and to revise their generalisations, removing nagging doubts about the accuracy of their impressions about the data.[33]

3.3 Number of near misses identified

We defined 'near misses' as incidents in which:

- something could have gone wrong but has been prevented
- something did go wrong but no serious harm was caused.

In our study, social work practitioners reported a total of 60 examples of near misses . They also reported 15 examples of 'serious cases'.

3.4 Who identified them?

Table 4 outlines the position of practitioners within the organisations. Due to time constraints, not all respondents were asked to identify near misses, but of those that were, the examples of near misses that they came up with were distributed across the three locations. We have excluded examples from the group interview because the positions of respondents are unknown. Four examples were identified in the group interview; hence 56 examples came from individual interviews. Examples were evenly distributed across both genders. The majority of respondents asked were white (52), identifying 51 near misses. Of the five black and minority ethnic respondents, four identified five near misses.

Examples of near misses were not, however, distributed equally across respondents. On analysis, this has proved to be related to their professional position. Two thirds of all examples (48/56) reported were identified by those at the forefront of the service: social workers, student social workers and managers. All the team managers and team leaders gave examples of near misses. This appears to reflect their position in terms of the management of practice: part of their role necessarily involves identification and management of near misses. Just under half of all examples (27) were identified by social workers, again reflecting their role in risk assessment and working directly with children and families and with other agencies. This suggests that the frontline is a fertile source of knowledge about safeguarding incidents.

Two of the service managers (of the three interviewed) who were both asked to identify a near miss were able give an example of one. As one might expect, family support workers did not report examples of near misses, reflecting their limited role in decision-making. The information and referral officer reported one example – a case where, when the officer dropped in some information to a service user, it was found that the police had failed to let social services know that her violent partner had been released on bail. The information and referral officer found the man in the house and was able to have him rearrested for breaking his bail conditions.

Senior managers, including quality assurance managers, identified a small number of examples (7). Where examples were identified by this members of this group, in almost all cases it was because an external agency had brought the example to their attention. This indicates a problem in terms of organisational learning from frontline practice, and will be discussed further in Chapter 8. It may also indicate a tendency to focus on active rather than latent failures, overlooking the role that senior decision-makers play in preventing error.[18]

Table 4: Positions of practitioners who gave examples

Position	Number of respndents	Total respondents asked	Number of near miss examples
Information and referral officers	01	01	01
Family support workers	02	02	00
Student social worker	02	02	04
Frontline practitioners	22	21	27
Team leaders	04	03	06
Team managers	06	06	06
Service managers	03	02	02
Quality assurance managers	04	03	05
Senior managers	07	07	02
Allied professionals	05	05	03

3.5 Safeguarding incidents

The numbers of near misses identified in our study, as discussed above, suggest that they are significant phenomena within children's services. This raises questions about whether an exclusive focus on 'serious cases' alone is adequate to any organisational risk management strategy. Yet there is no current language to capture the *range* of adverse incidents that happen within children's services, including those where no harm is caused. There is as yet no formal recognition or identification of near misses.

In healthcare, by contrast, the NPSA has developed the term 'patient safety incident' (PSI) to describe any unintended or unexpected incident that could have or did lead to harm for one or more patients receiving NHS-funded care.[34] This definition incorporates incidents that have been prevented or which occurred but no harm was caused, commonly referred to as 'near misses'.[2,35] These have been defined by the NPSA as 'prevented patient safety incidents' or 'no harm patient safety incidents'[2,34,36] respectively.

> We are trying to push the 'none event' reporting because it's a good way of learning. People call it the 'phew factor', which is 'Phew! It didn't go wrong so I don't feel so bad about life in general,' and they feel able then to talk to their friends about it and their colleagues – it's a *nice* feeling: 'I prevented this from happening but what if I didn't?' So we're really trying to promote that learning.
>
> *Director, National Patient Safety Agency*

Risk management within healthcare is concerned with the degree of harm caused by an incident, in order to eliminate or minimise the harmful effects of incidents.[36-38] 'Harm' is defined as injury, suffering, disability or death,[34] and PSIs are graded according to the degree of harm they cause. Like social work with children, risk is strongly associated with the potential for harm and is therefore a negative concept.[37-39] The grading of PSIs, however, also allows for positive outcomes arising from risk. The inclusion of a category for 'no harm' incidents or near misses by the NPSA enables incident records to be balanced with positive outcomes.[40]

Our study indicates the existence of near misses within childcare social work. There seems to be a case, therefore, for developing a new term to capture the *range* of incidents that happen within children's services, including those where no harm is caused. Patient safety is at the heart of healthcare services, while safeguarding children is a key objective of children's services.[41] Hence, we tentatively propose that the equivalent of a 'patient safety incident' in social care is a 'safeguarding incident'.

A 'safeguarding incident' results in harm or potential harm due to professional agencies' failure to keep a child safe, rather than from neglect or abuse by family members, for example. Like a 'patient safety incident', a 'safeguarding incident' also covers near misses that have the potential to lead to serious harm but have been prevented or have occurred but no serious harm was caused. A 'safeguarding incident' refers to an action combined with a potential or actual negative outcome.

Transferring initiatives from health to social care necessitates caution. 'Harm' manifests quite differently in children's services compared to healthcare. Childcare social workers are tasked with preventing both immediate and *long-term* harm. Consequently, grading safeguarding incidents within children's services is far from simple, and the health model developed by the NPSA proves to be of limited help. Table 5 below presents first steps towards developing a grading system for adverse incidents in children's services. Capturing longer-term consequences of interventions, or lack of them, requires wide consultation and debate. Crucially, it is also clear from the discussion in Chapter 4 that practitioners, young people and parents have different understandings of what constitutes harm, meaning that what are described as 'no harm' or near misses by social workers may be experienced as damaging by service users and carers.

Table 5: Grading of safeguarding incidents in children's services

Grade	Definition
No harm	• Any safeguarding incident that had the potential to cause harm but was prevented, resulting in no harm to children. • Any safeguarding incident that occurred but no serious harm was caused to children.
Harm	Safeguarding incidents that are harmful include false negatives (leaving a child in danger as a result of which the child is seriously harmed) and false positives (inaccurately assessing a family as dangerous).
Life-threatening injury or death	Any safeguarding incident that leads to a child dying, suffering a life-threatening injury or being seriously sexually abused, where local agencies have known that abuse or neglect is a factor and the case gives rise to concern about inter-agency working to protect children.

There are three grades of safeguarding incidents: 'no harm', 'harm' and 'life-threatening injury or death'. 'No harm' refers to near miss scenarios whereby something could have gone wrong but has been prevented or something did go wrong but no serious harm was caused. The category of 'harm' includes both false negatives (leaving a child in danger and the child is seriously harmed) and false positives (inaccurately assessing a family as dangerous). There is a tendency to focus on the former at the expense of acknowledging the pain and trauma caused to families by false positives. A series of recent high-profile cases involving parents wrongfully convicted of the murders of their children remind us how persistently professionals can cling on to an adverse opinion of a parent despite weak evidence.[19]

As noted at the beginning of this chapter, the final category currently receives most systematic attention within children's services. These safeguarding incidents involve death or life-threatening injury or injury through sexual abuse, even though local agencies knew that abuse or neglect was a factor, which gives rise to concern about inter-agency working to protect children.

Such cases are reviewed by ACPCs under the government guidance outlined in *Working together to safeguard children*,[32] known widely as 'part 8 reviews' or 'serious case reviews'.

It should be noted that these categories are not mutually exclusive: 'no harm' incidents may involve false positives as well as false negatives, while safeguarding incidents that are harmful may result tragically in death.

3.6 Conclusions

'No harm' incidents or near misses are common features of frontline practice in children's services. They represent a crucial opportunity to identify weaknesses within safeguarding systems before children are moderately or, more seriously, severely harmed. We suggest, therefore, that risk management strategies require a broader scope that focuses on near misses as well as serious cases.

To that end, a new language is needed that incorporates the whole range of adverse incidents that occur. We propose the term 'safeguarding incident' to capture the range of seriousness from 'no harm' incidents through to child death. We have outlined a simple grading system to be used. However, refining this model to incorporate both immediate and long-term harm, as well as appreciating differences in how social workers and service users understand harm, requires considerable consultation and further work.

4 Risk, need and near misses

4.1 Introduction

In this chapter, we present a more qualitative analysis of the data, which allows us to build a more detailed picture of the nature of near misses. We present case studies from social workers and their managers, highlighting the perspectives of parents and young people. From their examples and commentary, we pick out issues identified as playing a role in their occurrence.

We acknowledge, however, that the cases we present are almost exclusively examples of active rather than latent failures,[15] focusing on errors in frontline practice. This emphasis on active failures is a reflection of our focus on frontline staff, service users and carers rather than senior managers. Similarly, we acknowledge that examples tend emphasise false negatives rather than false positives. This may reflect the way that frontline staff conceptualise errors, which is driven by fear of being blamed. What are presented in this chapter, therefore, are largely cases where something could have gone wrong, but warning signs have been recognised and the situation retrieved.

The chapter begins with a brief introduction to the responsibilities of referral and assessment teams, highlighting the centrality of assessment of need. It then moves from the general context within which our study showed near misses to occur, to issues of particular significance to their occurrence as raised in the study by social workers, service users and carers.

4.2 Assessing need, prioritising immediate harm

The two guiding principles at the heart of the Children Act are: (1) protecting children from significant harm, and (2) promoting long-term welfare.[32] The Children Act 1989 introduced the concept of significant harm as the threshold that justifies compulsory intervention in family life to promote the best interests of the child.[41] Councils with social services responsibilities (CSSRs) have a duty to ensure that children are protected from significant harm. They also have a general duty to safeguard and promote the welfare of children in need of support beyond that of mainstream health and social care services.

Following the introduction of the Children Act 1989, the Department of Health (DH) commissioned a series of research studies to look at its implementation. This programme of research reported an over-emphasis on issues of abuse and neglect at the expense of assessing and supporting children in need. This approach was frequently experienced by families as traumatic and, unless suspicions of abuse were substantiated, rarely resulted in support services.[42,43]

This led to the debate on how best to 'refocus' services from the preoccupation with risk of significant harm towards a more holistic approach that considered the full range of children's developmental needs and circumstances.[44] The Assessment Framework, which came as a response to these findings, provides professionals with a conceptual framework 'for gathering and analysing information about all children and families, but [which] discriminated effectively between different types and levels of need'.[45]

In the current study, however, 'risk of immediate harm' continues to predominate the landscape within children's services. Indeed, the focus was on specific types of harm: children who are deemed at risk of physical or sexual abuse (i.e. immediate harm) cause more concern than those who are potentially at risk of neglect or emotional abuse.

The dominance of immediate harm over concerns about long-term welfare may reflect:

- continuing over-emphasis on risk at the expense of children in need
- media attention on child deaths and a culture of naming and shaming
- thresholds for intervention developed by agencies
- the difficulty of assessing neglect and emotional abuse
- a lack of professional confidence about how to work with children and families.

Assessing the needs of children, including the need to safeguard them from significant harm, has become a major preoccupation in social work.[46] There is a wealth of literature about to how assess children in need of safeguarding. A series of recent reviews provides helpful ways of understanding risk and uncertainty.[3,45-55] Some of this literature adopts a quasi-scientific angle, using the mathematics of probability as the starting point to develop an actuarial model to assist with the task of predicting outcomes.[54,56-59] Even those who favour this model, however, acknowledge its limitations in the field of child welfare and protection and suggest that it is difficult to predict events with any degree of accuracy. As Munro points out, 'it is surprisingly hard to develop a high accuracy rate in predicting a relatively rare event.[50] This is supported by Calder who argues that 'what is clear is that it is mighty difficult to develop any predictive instrument with a high degree of accuracy in child protection.[51]

This is a position adopted by many commentators: assessing risk of harm is not an exact science and probably the most we can hope for is best estimates.[55] Jones argues that risk assessment 'is simply too imprecise and inexact to apply in this field [child protection]. However, that is not to say that risk of future harm cannot be managed in a sensible, logical and open manner.[52] Indeed, research conducted by Jones suggests that what is known about risk factors in a population of children does not necessarily translate into understanding the risk to particular children within their family context.

> Risk takes many forms and the risk is very much dependent on the situation. You cannot have one definition of risk, because, as with everything to do with human beings, one definition does not fit all.
>
> *Social worker*

This complexity is noted by both practitioners and theorists alike. In all areas, prediction is difficult to achieve with any degree of accuracy, and this is particularly true with regard to assessing risks to children. The situation is compounded by the fact that risk factors are often cumulative, and longitudinal studies have demonstrated how difficult it is to predict long-term outcomes.[63] This has particular significance for social workers who are attempting to assess emotional abuse and neglect, which by definition take place over a substantial period of time.

The focus on assessment tools, procedures and related training as a means to unify understandings of risk at the expense of developing forums for discussion and having time for reflection has been increasingly questioned, however.[9,25,52] Parton argues that these developments are further consolidated with the increased reliance on information and communication technology (ICT) as means to structure assessments.[52] He suggests that such developments belong to a 'technological culture' where reflexivity is no longer about carefully considered decision-making: 'instead it is about the reflexive tying of knowledge to action, so that there is no distance at all between knowledge and action.' The focus is on action or operationality – 'what works' – rather than considering questions such as 'Why?' and 'Is there meaning to it?'[53]

Increasingly the reliance on narrative knowledge – where the emphasis is on constructing a coherent story and where the professional is seen as key in piecing this together – is being replaced by categorical knowledge where thinking is based on binary either/or logic that puts people or objects into categories, and where ambiguity is obscured. In categorical thinking, you tend to go down a list, choosing between various categories, but you must choose one. Each question narrows the choice of the next one so that thinking becomes algorithmic. Such an approach fails to grasp the importance of context, and that actions are mediated by circumstances that change over time and place. Categorising human identity into axis grids and risk instruments has the effect of taking unique, whole individuals apart and then putting them into the requirements of the various risk assessment tools, procedures and structures. Parton concludes that such instruments are not so much instruments for *understanding* but instruments for *action* or, as Lasch describes it: 'They owe less to meaning than to operation.'[52,53]

It is within this context that referral and assessment teams within children's services judge whether cases meet the threshold for intervention from social services and then decide how best to take cases forward. Indeed, there are specific performance indicators for children's services that define a timetable for action.[45] While there is a clear case for making decisions quickly and getting on with the job of safeguarding children, it is within this fast-paced, demanding, complex world of decision-making about risk of harm that cases have to be prioritised and then allocated to specific social workers.

4.3 Near misses arising during referral and assessment

Our study found that near misses often occurred during this referral and assessment phase. Our analysis showed that the misinterpretation or misdiagnosis of risk is a key feature of safeguarding incidents in general and near misses in particular. This indicates the difficulties of assessing risk at the expense of assessing and resourcing the needs of children. This means that many near misses involve cases where actual or potential significant harm to children has been overlooked, or where intervention has been left too late because needs have not been addressed. In other cases, workers may misjudge or overestimate the risks posed by a family to their child/children.

Three case examples from our study demonstrate this point. They illustrate the uncertainty, ambiguity, complexity and urgency that inevitably mark the work of those whose task is safeguarding children.[25,46,51] They also show diligence and determination on behalf of workers to ensure that children's needs have been met and that they are protected from harm.

Case: A seven-year-old girl was referred to social services by the fire service. She had been taken to them by her parents to 'teach her a lesson' about fire-setting [behaviour often associated with sexual abuse]. The referral was not prioritised and remained unallocated. Two months later, a second referral came from the girl's school, concerning a 10-day-old burn on her hand. The child had explained her injury variously as a carpet burn and as a scratch from her mother. A home visit found the family living in squalor. This led to a child protection conference, both because the burn itself was significant and because of the chronic neglect. Subsequently, following intuitive suspicions about the father, a very experienced worker picked up the case. Determined, she managed to locate 'missing' old files. These revealed significant earlier allegations of sexual abuse, which provided a key to understanding the dynamics of the situation.

Group interview, referral and assessment team

Case: This referral involved the mother's drug misuse and potential neglect. The mother had a new boyfriend who, on the surface, had made a good initial impression on the social worker. He appeared honest about previous misdemeanors, including burglary. The social worker's gut feeling, however, left her feeling sceptical. On returning to the office, she looked him up in the ICT system to ensure that the service had a full and accurate picture of all the information. On the system, she found that someone had written: 'Be very careful about this man. Don't visit him at home on his own.' Unsure if this was the same man, she called the family. Speaking to the mother, she said: 'I'm just doing this family tree of you. Can you just give me all the kids' names and dates of birth again, so I've got them right? Oh, and your boyfriend, what's his date of birth too?' She got the information by artifice, but she confirmed that the mother's boyfriend had, in fact, served 15 years for rape and indecent assault of a child.

Service manager

Case: A family came to social services' attention as European Union (EU) nationals with problems of financial hardship. The case was dealt with 'on face value'. It was allocated to an inexperienced worker who did not reassess the situation when she learned of parental mental health issues and signs of chronic neglect. The family did not return to social services. This triggered concerns from the team manager who made a decision to do a follow-up home visit. The worker found the mother unconscious and the family living in appalling squalor and evidence of long-term neglect.

Group interview, referral and assessment team

Assessing the needs of children will never be an exact science, and social workers will always have to prioritise some child protection cases over others. Yet on closer analysis, from the perspectives of both referral and assessment teams and young people and parents with experience of their services, certain issues were particularly significant in the occurrence of near misses. These included:

- the prioritisation of immediate harm at the expense of early intervention
- problems with accessing information
- difficulties at the interface between agencies
- the need to assess and re-assess long-term cases.

We address each of these in more detail below.

4.4 Prioritising immediate harm over early intervention

Despite efforts to refocus children's services away from a preoccupation with risk of significant harm towards supporting families to meet the needs of their children, the risk of immediate harm continues to take priority. In many of the case examples, the needs of children had been overlooked or resources were not available until risk of immediate harm was apparent. Indeed, the focus was on specific types of harm: children who were deemed at risk of physical or sexual abuse (i.e. immediate harm) caused more concern than those who were potentially at risk of neglect or emotional abuse. This was an issue that both service users and practitioners linked to near misses as well as to more serious adverse incidents. We deal with them consecutively.

4.4.1 Service user and carer perspectives on thresholds for intervention

In particular, parents with experience of using children's services identified the prioritisation of immediate harm over early intervention as a key factor in the occurrence of near misses.

> The thing is, in my situation, because he's not an abused child – I'm not hitting him, I'm not an alcoholic, I'm not a drug addict – he's not a priority. But that doesn't help me. There's all kinds of abuse. At the moment, he's abusing himself, you know. But at the end of the day, he is still a child in need.
>
> *Parent, group interview*

Parents felt that they were not taken seriously when requesting help; they felt they were 'palmed off' or simply ignored, not even offered an assessment when what they requested required support with the parenting role. This caused them immense frustration. One parent encapsulated the point by stressing that people only seek help from social services when they are desperate. Consequently, the importance of being treated with respect and understanding must not be underestimated.[64]

The parents explained the different thresholds for intervention between themselves and social workers in terms of their mutually different priorities. As they saw it, social workers focus on immediate risk of harm while they worry about long-term consequences.

> *Respondent 1*: They need to see the weight of it. Just because he's not lying there covered in blood. I mean, I'd like to see the written paper, what's the scale so that I can phone up and say: 'Number 2, please come and do something now!'?
> *R2*: That's right. Had to be an emergency. Because they'll continually say it: 'Well, we can't come today because there's an emergency.' And you're like, 'Well, what is an emergency to you? Because this is an emergency for me, and I need you here now!'

R3: But social workers need to see that, what your emergency is. And it's not just 'cause we're being silly – the child's at risk ... And that's what they don't see, and that hurts.

Parents, group interview

In their commentary, parents identified resource rationalisation and paperwork as key factors in determining that children at risk of immediate harm were prioritised over those whose circumstances appear less serious – or in other words, were prioritised over a wider focus on whether a children's needs were being met. Parents felt that limited resources and the pressure to close cases undermined the ability of children's services to respond to the priorities of families.

Yet they also highlighted that this bias led to situations where people were not getting the help they needed, without which situations not only could but did deteriorate and risk increased. In many of the examples they gave, family breakdown had resulted: 'Social services never took us seriously, and now he has had to go into care. If we'd got help when we asked for it, maybe things would not have come to this.'

Young people in care also felt that their family situations had been left to deteriorate without the necessary support or, in some cases, active intervention to protect them. In one example, a young person described witnessing the brutality of their violent father and the failure of social services to recognise the seriousness of the situation. Although not attacked physically, the young person described living in fear of their father and the relief of eventually being taken into care.

Interviewer: But given that you were, sadly for you, living in that situation, could something have been done, do you think?
R1: They could have like ...
R2: ... prioritised protection.
R1: Yeah, they could have like had a word with me like, by myself, and got me out.

Young people, group interview

4.4.2 Practitioners' reflections on risk, need and near misses

We stated earlier that examples of near misses described by respondents related to a risk of immediate harm to children often involved cases where needs had not been recognised or where resources were not available to meet those needs. The focus was on children deemed at risk of physical or sexual abuse, not on those potentially at risk of neglect or emotional abuse – cases that often became near misses. The tension involved in addressing both this aspects in their work was not one that the respondents in our study were complacent about.

I think we respond well to children who have an injury or where there's a disclosure because it's very clear cut and it's safe. Those are the areas that it's easy to work with. But it's the neglect issues – I think they're the ones that keep you awake at night because how far is too far? How bad is not good enough? It's the much more in-between areas that are very difficult.

Quality assurance manager

Like parents, practitioners were also well aware of the cost of prioritising immediate harm over early intervention. As one respondent noted about not intervening earlier in certain cases, for example, 'Yes, they've been damaged emotionally as well. There's been a cost to them of something not happening.'

When it came to doing anything about this skewed prioritisation of cases, however, our study revealed a prevalent feeling among practitioners that their hands were tied by an organisational focus on crisis intervention.

> I recognise that today's child in need is tomorrow's possible child in need of protection, and I think that, in a crisis intervention sometimes, because of the pressure, we go out there and assess and are not allowed to work for long term, to actually put in the supports to minimise that risk to a level that it's not going to happen again.
>
> *Team manager*

This point is also made by two newly qualified social workers:

> *R1*: If we had the time to be proactive rather than reactive, we would avoid them becoming children at risk. And quite often they are at risk when we get them, but if we had been able to get them earlier, we would have been delaying a need to protect them.
> *I*: So you think if you could do some preventative work as opposed to intervention … ?
> *R2*: Or both.
> *R1*: Yeah, I mean, obviously there's a need for both.
> *R2*: I think what the researcher's trying to say is that we do need to be doing more preventative work. And as we be more preventative, the actual child protection bit will go down.
>
> *Social workers*

At the moment, the Assessment Framework is the primary means of assessing children in need of protection. In the current study, concerns were raised about inconsistencies in practice in assessing such needs and ensuring resources were in place.[45] The new approach to information sharing and assessment is the Common Assessment Framework (CAF), which will be launched in 2005/06 (for more information, please visit www.everychildmatters.gov.uk/deliveringservices/caf/).

Both service users and practitioners identified the prioritisation of immediate harm over early intervention as a key issue in the occurrence of near misses specifically and safeguarding incidents more generally. There was some overlap in how they understood the reasons for this weakness in service provision.

4.5 Near misses involving problems with accessing information

Many young people and parents in our study argued that partial information was a key factor in near misses as well as in more serious safeguarding incidents. Service users and carers identified many examples of social workers not listening, failing to get the full picture, misinterpreting what was said or taking down inaccurate information.

Of particular concern, from their perspective, was that they are marginalised in the assessment process. They felt that they had little opportunity to comment on, let alone challenge, social workers' judgements, yet they questioned the accuracy and interpretation of information. They felt strongly that, as a direct result, mistakes were made. Previous research has also highlighted that families often disagree with the judgements made by social workers, but feel that they have few opportunities to challenge decisions made by professionals.[65] The following example was given by one of the parents involved in the study.

> When we had one-to-one direct contact with the social worker, an assessment was done in a more direct way so we were sat down with the social worker discussing our views and our opinions. We felt at that point empowered again. We felt that this was our opportunity to get across our point of view and we were acting on behalf of my daughter at the time. And we felt that this was a really positive thing. However, when that was transmitted into the form of a report, we didn't feel that that report reflected the assessment that happened during that time. At no point was the report checked out with us. We had the interview, we assumed that the social worker was putting down the right information. But it wasn't until we read the report – and, in fact, until it was too late and the courts were involved – that we realised that things had been missed or misrepresented or, in some cases, completely made up. We felt very let down by this process, but didn't seem to have any way of putting it right.
>
> *Parent, individual interview*

More generally though, young people and parents felt strongly that it was due to a lack of time and resources that social workers often did not access all the relevant information, thus heightening chances of safeguarding incidents. Many were sympathetic to social workers who they saw as overworked, bogged down in paperwork, undervalued and under siege. This is illustrated in the following commentary:

> There is not enough of them, so you phone up with something really urgent, but there is not enough of them in the office, so that means that they don't get time to get round and see what is going on in young peoples' lives. So they complain about that, but it's not your fault and it's not their fault either.
>
> *Young person, group interview*

> I don't think they have enough time in the day to listen, to really listen to what people want, what the people have to say about things. I don't think that that's the fault really of the social workers. There aren't enough of them for the amount of problems that there are today. And also because they haven't got enough time to spend with people – that's when you find mistakes being made. They are not able to give you the information that you want, and nine times out of ten, they don't want to give you it, because it means paper work.
>
> *Parent, group interview*

Young people and parents asserted that adequate time was necessary for social workers to access the relevant information so as to minimise the chances of near misses occurring. They also stressed such problems were exacerbated by the high turnover of staff. From their perspective, both accessing and interpreting information correctly required consistency of personnel in order for mutual trust and understanding to be feasible.

They literally are changing all the time and so you've got no one to really trust. The social workers don't know you. The social workers used to know you and your family, they used to know your family, you know, but now they don't know you, you're just a number.

Young person, group interview

Social workers and their managers also identified the theme of accessing information as relevant to near misses. Sometimes it was an issue of where the files were located that caused the access problem. In one case, this was because files were located in rat-infested cellars, so administrators were (understandably) reluctant to retrieve them. In another case, the moving of files from where the referral and assessment team was located into another building also created delays in their retrieval.

And we currently have a part 8 review, and one of the things they are going to look at is the delay in strategy meetings, 'cause it took two days to get the files and I wasn't happy to do it until I had the background. But I will have a pummelling about that.

Team manager

In other cases, practitioners identified ICT systems as the cause of problems with the access to information necessary to avoid mistakes. In one ICT system, it was impossible to alter details once they had been entered on the system. In a child protection case conference that we observed, the report contained inaccurate and incriminating details about the family that could not be corrected. An addendum had been added to the file, but there was concern among the practitioners involved that future workers would miss this. They feared that this would result in mistakes being made due to inaccurate information.

Other workers commented on the potential for mistakes happening because of the Eurocentric nature of ICT systems, which recognise only European name spellings. As a result, it was often difficult to identify children and families known to social services, with obvious implications for social workers' assessment of risk to the children concerned. In the case examples given, near misses had been averted because workers, who had been in the area for a long time, remembered the names of families and suggested that the ICT systems be searched again.

The two cases above represent good examples of latent failure. Given the known error rate even in the simple task of data-entry, this factor seems a latent failure of major significance. It is also difficult to see how frontline workers on their own could create adequate safety mechanisms to neutralise it. For instance, adopting a policy of only entering data once the assessment has been thoroughly checked would reduce but not eradicate error and could have its own adverse effects in being labour-intensive (requiring double recording of information) and in delaying the sharing of information with others via the computer system.[19]

Moreover, it is not simply a case of accessing the correct information; time needs to be given for information to be analysed, interpreted and reflected on. Lack of time may create latent failures whereby risk is missed or misinterpreted at the expense of children and families.

In other cases given by respondents, there were multiple causes for the lack of information available to social workers. In the following example, these included new workers, missing files and a lack of chronology. This case also demonstrates that problems accessing information can result in more than one near miss. Interestingly, the series of near misses in this case were highlighted by a guardian *ad litem* in court. The case also shows the importance of experienced social workers who have worked in the same area for a long time, know the families and are able to spot risks and intervene.

> Case: Serious concerns had been expressed about the safety of a child. The mother and child then went missing. Missing files, a poor chronology and workers new to the case meant that, when the mother and child did come into contact again with children's services, child protection concerns were not picked up. This happened on numerous occasions. By coincidence alone, a team leader who knew the history of the case took a referral about the family and ensured that an emergency protection order was made.
>
> *Team manager*

Participants in our study shed light on the ways that the issues involved in prioritising risk of immediate over long-term harm and the problems in accessing relevant information play a part in near misses happening in children's services. A third theme that arose from our analysis was the role played by allied professionals, including the police and the immigration and health services.

4.6 Near misses and the role of allied professionals

Successive government guidance has stressed that the task of safeguarding and promoting the welfare of children is a joint responsibility.[32] Many allied professionals, specifically teachers and general practitioners, have contact with a universal or near universal child population. In many of the examples given by respondents in our study, near misses had occurred due to decisions made by these allied professionals, as well as other agencies such as the police and the immigration and health services. Below, we present three such cases, the first two again highlighting the importance of early intervention and parenting support as a means of preventing safeguarding incidents.

> Case: A referral came from a post-natal hospital unit concerning a drug-using mother with learning disability. Her likely need for support to parent had not been picked up by the hospital at the prenatal stage and concerns were only voiced once the baby was born, so no pre-birth assessment had been completed. The referral was made on a Friday afternoon and a visit was made to the ward. Following checks with the health visitor and antenatal services, the baby was allowed home. Subsequent assessment at home found that the mother had left the three-day-old baby home alone and unfed for an estimated eight hours. The baby was placed in police protection.
>
> *Team leader*

Commentary: It's about risk again because ultimately it was seen as social services' decision to let [the mother] to go home. But the assessment hadn't really started, and at the time of discharge, it seemed OK to let her go because we had nothing else to go on. In hindsight, I would probably have prompted the worker to do further negotiations with the hospital. We just sort of let her go home without really challenging that, I suppose, [but] it was the first time [the worker] had to do an assessment, make a decision like that. It's quite emotional – people see him/her walking out the front door with a newborn baby and the mother screaming and shouting – so I think everyone can learn from the experience.

Team leader

Case: There were concerns that a child was at risk of neglect from long-term drug-using parents. The social worker requested that the police take out a police protection order for the child. On seeing the child, who was smiling, the senior officer described the child as 'happy enough' and refused. The social worker then made a voluntary agreement with the mother to place the child with the maternal grandmother. The court subsequently granted an emergency protection order.

Social worker

Commentary: 'I've seen worse' was another comment he [the police officer] said to me. And yes, he'd seen worse and the child looked happy enough 'cos the child was smiling even though the child was half naked. [It] was just beyond belief. I'm this child's social worker. I've been working with him six months. I'm telling you that this is not a safe environment for this child. So that was hard. I felt that I had done as much as I could, and if anything were, unfortunately, to happen to the child, then the blame would have laid on the police's door.

Social worker

Case: A child was brought into the country on a false passport by her alleged uncle. This man later left the country, but the immigration service failed to stop him and remove his passport, which was needed for evidence. This case was known to the immigration service, yet they said that they had not received information from social services in time. It was not clear whether the man had taken the child with him. There was also concern that the child has been sexually abused by the same uncle and was on the verge of disclosure. The school she attended was contacted, but they refused to tell the social worker whether the child was in school that day. The social worker sat for two hours waiting for this child but to no avail. On returning to the office, a colleague with a better working relationship with education called the school and found out that the child was indeed there. Subsequently the child was placed into foster care.

Social worker

Commentary: On that particular day it would have been helpful if the school had worked along with us, in the sense of they knew the situation, what was going on. But only when I came back, someone else from the office called up, and they gave us the information to say that she was actually in school, but I couldn't get to her. I suppose it was the school that was holding that information back, which wasn't helpful.

Social worker

These three cases give an indication of the complexity of inter-agency and inter-professional working, showing that, in a situation where there should be a designated teacher responsible for child protection, communications and relationships can fall down.

The diversity of agency functions between social workers, the police, health personnel, mental health professionals, lawyers and teachers makes child protection an issue of greater or less familiarity and priority to each of them.[64]

The cases also hint at the enormous range of problems that can occur and potentially lead to near misses or more serious safeguarding incidents. Issues raised in these examples alone include personal hostilities, lack of respect for childcare social workers' professional specialisation and expertise, and unexplained breakdowns in communication as well as problems caused by passing concerns about a child's welfare over to social services at the last minute.

Research shows, however, that both teachers and general practitioners are unclear about their role in safeguarding children and about the appropriate procedures.[49] Moreover, allied professionals are often uncertain about what constitutes risk to children. Research suggests that they have lower tolerances about the level of risk to children.[66-68] Respondents' commentaries indicate a keen awareness of how issues of trust, communication, collaboration and understanding between agencies and professionals are linked to potential mistakes.[32,49]

Allied professionals also provided examples of near misses: some were about social services not taking their views about risk of harm to children seriously, while others described cases where risk had been missed by their own agencies. Conversely, however, service users and carers also provided examples in which allied professionals played a crucial role in averting near misses.

From the perspective of parents, social services are more likely to respond to requests from allied professionals than from family members.[59] One example from our study involved the mother of a child with attention deficit hyperactivity disorder (ADHD), who had requested window locks to prevent her son jumping from the window. Social services appear not to have fully assessed the needs of this particular child or accepted its resource responsibilities. Only following intervention from the housing department were locks fitted.

> ... and it got to the point where I was crying. And I went to the council in the end and I said to the council: 'I cannot cope with this no more. I have caught him hanging outside the window ledges today, hanging on for grim death, you know, screaming blue murder, 'cos he's a dainty little thing anyway, he'd have been broke to pieces.' I went to the health visitor and she suggested speaking to my housing manager. And the housing manager got on to the phone to social services and said: 'This is not on. If this is not provided, she will be going to speak to a solicitor.' And they then pulled their finger out. Within two weeks, I had window locks.
>
> *Parent, group interview*

4.7 Near misses and long-term cases

Many other examples of near misses from our study involved 'long-term' cases. These are cases that are either currently receiving support from social services, or have previously received support and are, therefore, known to childcare professionals. It is worth remembering that assessing need is not a one-off event – new information becomes available and situations change over time. This is why it is essential that social workers constantly review and possibly revise their judgements and decisions.[24,27] One theme that emerged in social workers' commentaries about near misses was the danger of complacency in long-term cases resulting in a greater likelihood that risks to children are overlooked.

> ... if you think Maria Colwell, Jasmine Beckford, Ricky Neave, some of the big ones, they have actually been about children who were known to everybody for a long time and where either there was some kind of deadening that went on in terms of people's ability to maintain involvement and interest. I mean, I suppose I'm just saying I think it's much easier to have your focus on the shiny new crisis than on the long-term drudge where it's all sticky and you don't feel you're getting anywhere and all the sort of things that slide in terms of the standards that are acceptable for this child that you wouldn't accept for another child that's a brand new one coming into the system.
>
> *Service manager*

However, respondents also argued that risks can be overlooked in long-term cases not because of complacency but because of a tendency to give people you know 'more leeway' than you would to those with whom you have had no previous involvement. This is demonstrated in the following case and related commentary.

> Case: Social services had been working with this family for many years, including looking after the children while the mother was in rehab recovering from drug addiction. After rehab, though, the mother replaced drugs with alcohol. There were drunken parties in her house. Neighbours, unhappy about the mother's behaviour, had attacked the house. Her request to be rehoused was refused. The concern was that the children were at risk from neglect. The social workers who know the mother were keen to keep the family together because she was caring and attentive and had been taking the children out on trips, and the children clearly loved their mother. They felt that they had seen a positive change in her parenting behaviour and an initial decision was made to leave two children in her care. The team leader reminded the workers of the 'rule of optimism' and advised caution in taking too rosy a view given the history. Subsequently, on finding the children home alone while the mother was out drinking, they were removed and taken into foster care.
>
> *Social worker*

> Commentary: There's probably lots of cases where ... it's not the danger of being too familiar with cases, but you can give people a lot more leeway if you've got some history going with them, or the teams have got a history going with them. So, I think some of the history things would give you that decision to say, 'Oh, let this person have a bit of a chance. I've seen such a change in them.'
>
> *Social worker*

Referral and assessment teams assess need, including the need to safeguard children from significant harm, and, where appropriate, refer cases on to other teams to manage such risks on a more long-term basis. The family support team therefore often has the difficult task of keeping alert to risks on long-term cases. This includes being alert to the need to assess and re-assess judgements about what is happening in various cases. A case example and accompanying commentary of such an incident follows:

Case: A child previously on the child protection register, whose case was being managed by the family support team, was re-referred to the referral and assessment team because of further concerns. These included depression, loss of hair and the delayed growth of the child. The case was taken to a second child protection conference where a decision was taken that the child needed to be removed. On attempting to take the child, the mother had barricaded herself in, and the child said to social workers: 'My mum's going to kill herself now.' There was fear that she would harm the child. An emergency protection order was sorted, the door knocked down and the mother restrained.

Team leader

Commentary: The risks were not being managed in this case. I think the family support team is traditionally a really difficult team to manage. I think it's really easy for long-term cases to lose their way unless you've got very focused management. For example, there are lots of risks that are unidentifiable – you know things aren't right, you have to keep on top of things.

Team leader

Other examples of near misses involving long-term cases highlighted the process of transferring a case from one team to another as a flash point for safeguarding incidents generally, including near misses. The following case exemplifies this issue and involves the handover of a case to the emergency duty team (EDT). It also raises EDT resource issues and skills development.

Case: The school referred a seven-year-old girl to social services. The family was known to social services because her mother had mental health problems and there were concerns about the little girl's welfare. It was known that her aunt was collecting her and taking her home. It was assumed at this point that the child was safe. A home visit was arranged but no one was home. EDT was contacted to do a home visit. In the meantime, the situation deteriorated and the mother threw the aunt out. The aunt contacted the police to say the mother had threatened the child with a knife and the child needed to be removed. EDT made a home visit, and the mother, though very unwell, was not deemed to be sectionable. The child was not seen during the visit. No intervention was made. When visited at school by a social worker the next day, the child confirmed that her mother had taken a knife to her throat and threatened to kill her. Understandably the child had been extremely frightened and had been delighted when the social worker called. She had already packed her bags and had been sitting in her bedroom waiting, expecting to be taken somewhere safe. The child was subsequently taken into care.

Team manager

Commentary: I mean, EDT, they're under-resourced. I think there needs to be a proper look at what is expected of them. I would have thought that, in a scenario like that, where they'd had forewarning of the case so they had information – it wasn't like a cold case, they knew the issues – there's a child there who's even packed her own bags, desperate to get out, and then they leave her there. I just think that's... that would be the bottom line, the first thing that somebody should do is talk to the child.

Team manager

Many of the issues raised above relate to reasons given by respondents in our study as to why risk of harm had been missed in long-term cases. Practitioners also pointed out that identification of such risk is not sufficient to avert harm – something also needs to be done about it. It also raises questions about early intervention and the support package offered to this child and her family. Cases such as these underline the importance of assessing needs, not solely the risk of significant harm, of resourcing robust family support packages and of focusing efforts on preventing family breakdown.

In others cases, where family support packages had been working, there was often difficulty in demonstrating to others that the degree and kind of risk had changed sufficiently to necessitate a different kind of intervention. One case involved a mother who used alcohol and whose daughter had suffered a series of accidental injuries due to poor supervision. A child-in-need plan was already in place and, despite the request of the child's social worker, health professionals did not judge the mother's bad supervision of her daughter extreme enough to meet thresholds for child protection intervention. The little girl was later found abandoned in the street by the police with the mother 'off her head'. Luckily, the child had suffered no serious injury.

4.8 Identifying underlying patterns of error

While this small-scale exploratory study primarily identifies active failures – those made by workers at the frontline – its findings are a rich source of possible underlying patterns or, at the least, hints of where to dig deeper to identify those patterns.[19]

Identifying the underlying patterns or the 'types' of errors that occur is a crucial step to devising solutions. Woods and Cook distinguish the surface description of an error (the phenotype) from the underlying patterns of systemic factors (the genotype).[69] The phenotype is unique to a particular setting. Genotypes reappear in many situations.

Genotypes are concepts and models of how people, teams, and organisations coordinate information and activities to handle evolving situations and cope with the complexities of that work domain.[70]

For example, the organisation of contemporary referral and assessment teams may create latent failures. On the one hand, a 'single point of entry' operated by the referral and assessment system works well to protect children where risk is obvious and urgent intervention needed. This contrasts with the past, where there were multiple points where referrals could be made in decentralised services and where local knowledge counted much for how risks were understood. Now, the referral and assessment service can often be a single team that covers a large authority that has little knowledge of local neighbourhoods and families. They deal with a large number of referrals and fast-moving events, offering swift intervention focusing on the most pressing concerns.

Therefore, it may take more time for less visible issues to come to the surface. This means that the referral and assessment system works well with those cases where indicators are clear, but those that do not cause immediate concern are missed by such a system or linger on the periphery and almost *have to become* a near miss in order to get picked up in a system that focuses on what can be sifted into a firm set of indicators warranting action. In other words, the organisation of the service can itself play an unintended part in the creation of latent failures or near misses.[71]

The management of time is also an indicator of the trade-offs being made at the frontline between the demands of different tasks and the relative priorities given to them. Parents, in particular, felt that pressure to complete assessments encourages cutting corners, with the attendant risk of making mistakes, while at the same time discouraging the types of activities – e.g. spending more time with the family – that would improve accuracy. It is possible that policy-makers' and senior management's perception of the time and tasks involved in good assessments is unrealistic and creates a latent failure. In other words, drivers to something – complete assessments – which are seen as the primary means of keeping children safe may be creating latent failures by pushing out other strategies for creating safety (e.g. spending time talking to the parents or child to check your information and assessment).[19]

4.9 Conclusion

In this chapter, we have highlighted the inherent complexity of assessing the needs of children, particularly the need to safeguard them from significant harm, which makes it impossible to guarantee total and consistent accuracy. Indeed, practitioners' commentaries show that near misses were a regular occurrence; in their experience, they were part and parcel of the job.

However, more detailed analysis of the examples of and commentaries about near misses, given by service users and practitioners alike, revealed a range of details particularly significant to their occurrence. In particular, many near misses identified by respondents in this study happened because the needs of children had been overlooked or not resourced, meaning that risk of harm had reached critical levels. However, many other near misses may involve defensive decision-making where risks to children have been over-estimated at the expense of working to support families.

Nevertheless, in laying out the examples given, we have begun to build a much more nuanced picture of the kinds of active failures that occur at the frontline and which suggest that latent failures are embedded in the system, including a lack of sufficient resources to meet the needs of children and their families.

5 Learning from near misses

5.1 Introduction

This small-scale research project has provided a unique insight into the occurrence of near misses in children's services. Near misses present an important means of learning from mistakes *before* serious harm is caused to children and their families. Through the examples they gave and their commentaries about them, practitioners and service users alike emerged as key sources of knowledge about the contexts within which near misses take place as well as about factors causal to their occurrence.

The increasingly complex picture we have built up about near misses in frontline children's services is based predominantly on the individual experiences of practitioners, young people and parents who took part in our study. The questions, therefore, arises as to whether opportunities currently exist for individuals to learn from their experiences. Moreover, given that 'free mistakes' represent such a strategic means of identifying and redressing weaknesses in the provision of child protection services, do opportunities exist for organisations to share the knowledge that people individually accumulate?

5.2 Learning organisations

The concept of a learning organisation has emerged from attempts to identify the key characteristics of successful companies and organisations in both the public and private sectors.[72-76] Pedler and Aspinall describe it as 'an organisation that facilitates the learning of all its members and consciously transforms itself and its context'.[74]

> The concept of learning organisations ... focused attention on the idea that not just managers as individuals, but organisations as corporate entities, could and should develop learning capabilities.[77]

One of the issues clearly identified by all those writing about learning organisations is the importance of learning from mistakes.[72-76] Within literature on how organisations learn, a series of necessary features have been identified.

SCIE has published a resource pack about learning organisations.[78] It provides summaries of research, describes ways to test out how well an organisation is doing at developing learning and gives guidance on how to move to a culture of learning in the workplace. It is based on the idea that informed decision-making can best take place in the climate of a learning organisation, and that good practice and opportunities for learning are inextricably linked. This includes learning from near misses. (To obtain a copy of the resource pack, visitwww.scie.org.uk/publications/learningorgs/index.asp.)

To capture the essential characteristics of a learning organisation, the SCIE pack uses a framework devised by Isles and Sutherland who applied it to the NHS.[76,78] They argue that there are five key features that are fundamental to a learning organisation:

- structure
- organisational culture

- information systems
- human resources practices
- leadership.

We have used these features to guide our analysis of factors that assist and inhibit learning from near misses as identified by respondents in our study. This five-part division, like all such tools, has its limitations. The main features of learning organisations overlap with and impinge on each other in multiple ways. Respondents, in their commentaries, often addressed more than one of these features simultaneously; sometimes they linked them causally. Consequently, we have not used the above categorisation of the features of a learning organisation strictly; we have refrained from imposing false divisions on respondents' commentaries.

5.3 Cultures of blame, climates of fear and issues of leadership

Learning organisations ideally have an organisational culture that:

- promotes openness, creativity and experimentation among members
- encourages members to acquire, share and process information
- provides the freedom to try new things, risk failure and learn from mistakes
- celebrates and shares good practice
- systematically gathers views from service users and carers and uses them to influence service planning
- creates opportunities for members to think and reflect and to learn from new evidence and research.

Organisations with the kind of culture described above are likely to capture and disseminate all learning – including, in principle at least, learning from near misses.

According to the practitioners in this study, however, rather than being a culture that fosters openness, an organisational culture of blame is prevalent in children's services, one that fosters a fear of talking about incidents that could have, or actually did, go wrong.

It is worth repeating that it is testimony to their commitment to the improvement of individual and organisational practice for service users and carers that practitioners were so open about their mistakes, despite concerns that to do so might be held against them. Yet none felt that transferring such openness about near misses from a small-scale study to the workplace would be easily accomplished.

Indeed, cultures that foster blame and create defensiveness could also be seen as types of latent failure. An unwillingness to admit to mistakes or to deviate from procedures, even when the case presents unique features that make the procedures inappropriate, can create circumstances in which errors are more likely. It is difficult to see how workers can learn from their experience if even supervision does not offer them the blame-free environment in which they can risk reflecting.[19] This means that, while respondents, in the main, fully endorsed the rationale of learning from 'free mistakes', the common fear of being blamed was seen as a major obstacle.

It's very difficult to do, in all honesty, and I think that's the downside of this system. My anxiety is that the social services reps in this group will begin to feel pressurised and overly defensive. And I understand that, but this is about developing the confidence of the individual within the organisation. As I say, we are human. We do make mistakes. Everybody makes mistakes. You need to be confident in yourself, within your teams, about what you can and can't do and be able to say, 'We've made a mistake. We should have done ABC&D instead of EF&G.' It's about promoting the culture to develop the confidence of individuals.

Quality assurance manager

Accounts highlighted the prevalence of a defensive attitude among staff resulting from the culture of blame surrounding the issue of mistakes. As the following extract indicates, social workers were often described as fearful of others finding out that their work was not always perfect.

Respondent: This is going to sound funny, but this is what I really think – people think: 'I don't want anyone to know what case I'm working on in case, if I get it wrong, they'll know it's me.' That's basically what I think, that is what I feel.
Interviewer: So people are afraid of being blamed …
R: Yeah, that's the sense of what I get.

Specialist social worker

Such defensiveness on the part of practitioners was often referred to as 'back covering' and was mentioned quite frequently. Practitioners and service users and carers explained this as, in part, due to the critical and unforgiving stand towards mistakes taken by the mass media.

I feel myself that the media has a lot to do with the bad feelings that people have towards the social services. And what we mustn't forget is that when, if they do something wrong and the media get hold of it, it is all flagged up. When they do something good, we don't hear anything about it.

Parent, group interview

Pertinently, the tendency to 'cover one's back' was often linked to issues of leadership both generally and at various specific levels. One respondent suggested that rhetoric from managers at 'upper levels' was often contradicted in reality.

I think the thing about blaming is a very mixed bag because some people say all the right things – i.e. 'This is about learning and not about blaming' – but the reality is, for some people, even if it's not overt to the individual worker or the individual team, at upper levels, it's there and it's thought about, you know. These people are deemed as incompetent, and they're never going to get promotions in this department.

Team manager

Another respondent described a conversation with their service manager about mistakes made in a certain case, in which they had talked explicitly about the need to think and act defensively, to make sure 'you cover your own back'. This experience was quite typical.

The service manager said to me last week, 'You have to cover yourself.' We were talking about a case where, you know, something hadn't been recorded at the time it had happened, about the decision-making ... So I said: 'Well [name of service manager], I could spend 100 per cent of me time covering me back side, you know.' They said, 'You *need* to cover yourself.' It was a kind of helpful comment in a way, but the implied threat was there. It's been said to me before: 'You are very exposed in terms of what you do, you know, your whole role, in terms of what you do, is exposed, you're the decision-maker, you know, so you need to cover yourself.' And I know what they meant.

Team leader

Many respondents commented on the need for a commitment to an open learning culture at all levels of the organisation if learning from near misses was to be feasible. They stressed that, currently in children's services, this was far from the case. Some had experienced resistance on the part of managers to even hearing about near misses and, therefore, remained sceptical.

These things will be problematic – it will not happen at the top level either – basic grade workers will not be able to say 'This went wrong' because managers do not want to know. As an individual, you could be as open as you like, but you need to have it collectively – that goes all the way down the line.

Social worker

No, you might on a peer level [voice concerns about cases], to mates in the office – but it is not encouraged by management at all. That might be something that happens, on occasion, individually with particular workers, but it is hidden in the team. Team leaders are well aware of what happens with every case. I suspect that, if there were close calls, they would not have been made public.

Social worker

That would be great, collective group learning from mistakes – but the management would prevent it. Where I worked, they were very autocratic, so nothing would filter through. Any safeguards which were drawn up would not be helpful. It would be the management's take on it – not the practitioner's.

Student social worker

Sometimes it was the local authority itself that was seen as perpetuating the fear of being blamed, compounded by attitudes evident in the media.

There is a climate of fear in all authorities, and there is a view that, if things go wrong, then they [frontline social workers] wouldn't be well supported. They would be treated like they'd done it themselves in that sense. That's partly about the media, but it's also about the messages that they give in the authority.

Team leader

Local authorities were seen as unsupportive of the open culture necessary for group learning from mistakes. One service manager commented that 'It's like *Yes, Minister* working in this authority.'

The individualistic attitude of 'looking after number one' and covering yourself was seen as the opposite of the culture within the health service. The respondent below felt that an open culture – one in which one could learn from safeguarding incidents – would not happen in social services because managers could not be relied on for support, whereas within the NHS, there was a culture of looking out for each other.

> The culture of the NHS is that they are prepared to look after their own – that does not happen in social work. There is a closing in of ranks in the health service. In social work, no manager will protect you as they will be too busy protecting themselves.
>
> *Student social worker*

If organisational learning depends on a specific kind of culture, the respondents in our study clearly indicated that the leadership in services to children and families was not necessarily supportive of that culture. Good leaders model the openness, risk-taking and reflection necessary for learning, and communicate a compelling vision of the learning organisation. They provide vision, and any attempts to learn from close calls and near misses would have to be sanctioned and supported by them. From the perspective of many (but not all) childcare social workers, current leadership encourages a culture of blame and a climate of fear that diminishes the actual learning or potential to learn from mistakes generally and from near misses in particular.

So what of the views of the people in positions of leadership who took part in our study? Frontline managers were clear that they wanted staff to discuss near misses. They fully endorsed open debate about what was happening on cases, particularly where situations had to be retrieved. Indeed, what concerned them was that staff would cover up mistakes instead.

Among senior managers, in contrast, there was discussion about the extent to which they needed to know about near misses at all, focusing on where it was best to address near misses. Some argued that it was better for cases to be dealt with locally, enabling learning to take place for specific areas.

Of particular concern to allied professionals was that learning be promoted across the boundaries of agencies and local authorities. They also wished to move away from a culture of blame, both of individuals and between agencies.

> I personally feel that the part 8 process is becoming accusatorial. It's important to keep the theme as learning from mistakes made, and not punishing people for mistakes they've made in the process. And that's difficult now because, as you said, scapegoating is the easiest thing in the world, especially for organisations, if they can say, 'It's not health's problem. It's social services that caused this problem.' So there's often the need to blame.
>
> *Senior police officer*

Issues of organisational culture and leadership formed one strong theme in respondents' talk about the actual and potential feasibility of learning from near misses in their work. Another theme that emerged from the data related to issues of organisational structure, to which we now turn.

5.4 Forums for discussion, time for reflection and a reporting system

Learning organisations have structures that both support teamwork and promote the development of lateral as well as vertical learning loops. This means that people learn from each other and from a variety of sources other than their managers. As well as from the team, there is important learning to be gained from service users and carers – whose views and perceptions have been highlighted throughout the current report – as well as from other professionals outside the team or, indeed, outside the organisation.[72,75]

Most of the respondents in the current study commented on the value that they placed on learning from other team members. This was particularly true for less experienced social workers, but whatever their experience, respondents emphasised the importance of sharing uncertainties with colleagues about particular decisions. Respondents also saw these team discussions as important informal learning opportunities.

> Fortunately for us, this is quite a stable team, and I think, although there is a lack of experience, if you look at the whole team there's still stability. The team has sort of grown together; a lot of the younger social workers grow together and learn off each other – sharing and talking about cases. I think people are quite good at talking to each other quite informally. We're that kind of team where people say, 'What about so and so with that case, with that family?' and you go, 'Oh, yeah.' So people do talk with their colleagues.
>
> *Senior practitioner*

> Sometimes, on duty, everyone becomes aware of what's going on. You have those cases – you know what's happening, what's this about. So I think other people would have learnt, not necessarily in a formal way but in an informal way ... I mean, it was just a crazy day and everyone chipped in. There was no one just in the duty team, everyone chipped in, and I think that's great for teams in a way, not because of the actual work but the way the teams come together and are supportive and see cases through really.
>
> *Team leader*

Informal discussions such as these were identified as prevalent across all the teams. Yet only in certain teams had this organisational learning mechanism been formalised into forums such as practice development meetings. Where this had occurred, these were identified as potential forums for close calls and near misses to be discussed routinely.

> Hopefully the practice development sessions will start to break that ice. We had one yesterday where people started bringing cases word for word, from the word go. So the fact that people have the option to have the case where they don't know where to go and discuss it with their colleagues and hopefully prevent close calls. Um, but then, by being able to discuss cases, people feel more relaxed, and they start accepting that people aren't going to blame them, or call them stupid, for missing something ...
>
> *Social worker*

In the view of the respondent quoted above, organisational structures such as formal forums for discussion would play a significant role in changing an organisational 'culture of blame' in which people are reticent about openly acknowledging mistakes.

Teams were commonly seen as supportive environments for talking about uncertainty involved in specific cases, but talking specifically about mistakes within teams was sometimes associated with the fear of being mocked. A respondent pointed out that this fear often prevents open discussion and was, therefore, a significant barrier to the potential for learning from near misses.

> Would you actually admit on the team basis that 'Hey, I cocked this one up. I made a mistake on it'? I think that probably, in that particular case, knowing the worker, I think they quite happily brushed it under the rug, marked it down to experience for them. So I think it is about getting over that barrier ... I don't know if the person involved would actually see it as a chance for the team to learn or just have a laugh.
>
> *Social worker*

Moreover, while many respondents made clear that various opportunities for learning from each other do exist within their organisations, a common theme was that these were far from systematic. Instead, the element of chance was identified as featuring strongly, with the result that much individual learning from cases, including near misses, was not likely to be shared with colleagues.

> *I*: How would learning from the case that you have mentioned be fed back in?
> *R*: At the moment, to be blunt, I don't think it would get fed back in. I think that's just a personal thing that might disseminated if (a) I'm talking to somebody about a case or (b) managers are talking to people about cases and they assessing: 'Oh, yeah, I remember that case' and 'Oh, that happened.' I wouldn't even know how to phrase it or whatever to disseminate it back in, so I think, while for me it was a good experience, I learnt a lot from it, [but] nobody else is going to learn anything.
>
> *Social worker*

If respondents highlighted the lack of systems in place for disseminating learning from practice generally, the lack of official forums in which to tackle near misses was particularly noted as inhibiting the potential for learning from them.

> I don't think there is a forum for that [learning from near misses]. I think that we all learn very much on an individual level. Between us, if we put all of our knowledge together, you've got every case covered, but individually it's ... unless something similar happens to you and you start talking to a colleague, and they say, 'Oh, have you tried this?' and you think, 'Oh yes.'
>
> *Social worker*

While recognising that some workers would probably find formal case discussions threatening, other respondents simultaneously pointed out that a major structural obstacle to learning from near misses was the lack of time set aside for it. A sense of frustration at the lack of organisational commitment to making time for such discussion is evident in the following extract.

I think we should do more formal case discussion. There are a few near misses that have cropped up in the last few months, and I've identified that they would be good learning points if we could have a small group of people involved in those cases – say, in the last six months – to get together to talk about them. I think some people might find that a bit threatening, but I would promote that more within the team, but of course, you always have to make time for those things.

Team leader

As well as the current lack of time in which to hold regular formal forums to facilitate group learning from near misses, there is also a need for time to reflect on one's personal work, including near misses when they occur. Many respondents were concerned that findings from the current study would lead to additional paperwork, when what was needed was time to think through decisions and whether things could have been done differently.

I suppose I got very exercised by the idea that what people need is not more guidance, it's not more procedures, it's not more memos saying 'Why aren't you doing things?', but actually time to chew things over, time for reflection.

Service manager

There was strong recognition among participants that some mechanism needs to be in place to support time for such thought processing and critical reflection, both individually and in groups, which can so easily get lost amid heavy caseloads.[79,80]

... you need the time to be able to process what you are doing and think about it and use it in your work, because if you're straight back from a really heavy case, you can't do it. So I think we'll be able to support that through the performance appraisals. We're not there yet, but at least it gives us the mechanisms to start doing it.

Quality assurance manager

The above discussion has focused on the structural issues of the lack of both forums and time in which to reflect on and learn from practice generally and from near misses in particular as they affect teams. Structural features to facilitate mutual learning between social work teams and service users or between social work teams and other agencies and allied professionals have been striking only in their absence. This reflects the fact that respondents did not indicate that forums for this kind of lateral learning currently exist. Neither did they feature within their horizons of possibility as a means of facilitating optimal learning from near misses. We will return to the issue of involving service users and carers shortly.

The lack of structural mechanisms to facilitate vertical learning from near misses, in contrast, did receive attention. In the previous section, we highlighted the fact that senior managers were perceived as not wanting to know about near misses. This perception is compounded by the current lack of mechanisms for reporting them. Consequently, senior managers who see the potential of using near misses to improve risk management have no structural means by which they can learn of their occurrence.

We don't have a reporting system, although I do increasingly think that should be the case. People should be encouraged rather than discouraged. Rather than just covering their back, people should be saying, 'We've got a problem here and we want somebody to unpack it with us and look at it.'

Service manager

Near misses that happen in frontline practice are invariability brought to the attention of senior managers by professionals from outside social services. Moreover, as indicated in the service manager's commentary above, respondents also highlighted the lack of support for ways of going about learning from near misses when they have been identified. This remains closed to all but serious cases, which, as we explained in Chapter 3, are referred to the Area Child Protection Committees (ACPCs).

There isn't a mechanism for us to put our hands up and say we've had a close call … Once a near miss is serious enough, it goes straight to the ACPC. Well, I think that, if you had another way of doing it that meant that it wasn't being dealt with at such a high strategic level – perhaps it was dealt with through another sub-group, a much smaller sub-group, or a different kind of sub-group – then I think people might feel more inclined to use that forum.

Service manager

5.4.1 Opportunities for involving service users and carers

During our study, no evidence surfaced of organisational forums for learning from near misses that involved service users and carers. There was no indication of any systematic methods for seeking feedback from service users and carers involved in near misses, about their views of why things went wrong or what could be done differently to prevent similar safeguarding incidents in the future. This is particularly worrying considering that, as discussed in Chapter 4, it was parents who had pointed out that social workers' prioritisation of immediate harm over early intervention often led to near misses or more serious safeguarding incidents.

Indeed, our research revealed that service users and carers commonly felt that they were actively prevented from finding out about near misses. Young people, in particular, felt that when mistakes were made, they were subsequently covered up. As many young people observed, 'When a mistake happens, it is covered up most of the time.'

I'm not sticking up for them, but they are just people. Everyone makes mistakes but you have to learn from them.

Young person, group interview

Not only did our study indicate the kind of knowledge that service users can uniquely bring to efforts to learn from mistakes, it also revealed that involving parents and young people would be far less problematic than practitioners might imagine. The service users in our study made it clear that they wanted an open approach towards mistake management. Moreover, analysis of their commentaries shows that they did not want this as a means of seeking retribution. They were not interested in joining in the blaming game.

I can't undo my disaster now. It happened. I'm in it. But if we can stop the same thing happening to a few other people, then I'm happy to help.

Parent, individual interview

Instead, services users and carers generally understood, and were sympathetic to, the pressures that social workers work under. Simultaneously, they by and large accepted that it will never be possible to have totally error-free services; they understood that mistakes will happen.

Of crucial importance to the service users and carers in our study was that safeguarding incidents are identified and acknowledged, that apologies are made to the children and families involved and that improvements take place. A recent study led by Professor Andy Pithouse at Cardiff University on advocacy and complaints by children to health, social services and education in Wales found similar findings. A common refrain of the 25 young people interviewed who had made a complaint to social services was 'Own up, apologise and move on'.[81]

I: If your social worker made a mistake, what would you like them to do?
R1: I'd like a written apology.
R2: Apology.
R1: In writing.
R2: And not do it again, learn from it.

Young people, group interview

They also stressed that an open approach to learning from safeguarding incidents, including near misses, would serve to restore trust in social services and help families begin to heal from what are often extremely painful experiences.

I'll never forget, I'll never forget what's happened to us. Not ever. It will stay with us for ever. Let's put it this way: I don't show very much emotion about it because I can't. I cannot, you know, ever. I can't really ever let go. Not ever. I've got to stay strong for my daughter, you know. But anything that will help save other people, who perhaps come across, not our circumstances 'cos they are quite unique, but a circumstance where people feel that they want answers. Anything that I can do to help other people, I will do.

Parent, individual interview

5.4.2 Conclusions

What has come to the fore through the opinions and reflections of social workers and their managers, service users and carers is the rejection of the culture of blame that they see as currently marking children's services. We have also shown the value that the social workers and their managers in the current study placed on learning from others in the organisation. Yet, in terms of organisational structure, both time and forums for learning specifically from near misses were lacking within teams. Moreover, mechanisms and forums that would include service users and carers or other agencies and allied professions in the learning process were striking only in their absence. The lack of a reporting system that would allow senior managers into the loop was also identified.

Overall, then, this chapter has shown that there was a paucity of evidence that learning from near misses currently takes place at an organisational level. It has also shown that the majority of people who took part in this study were individually supportive of the idea of learning from mistakes before harm is caused, but felt strongly that, due to organisational constraints, their hands remained quite firmly tied.

6 Conclusion and suggestions for the future

Risk management programmes that harness learning from adverse events and near misses have proved to be an important method of improving safety. This approach has been pioneered within aviation and, more recently, adopted by the healthcare sector within the UK.

> On this mistake management thing, there's a culture of shame around mistakes and that needs to be addressed at its core. My teacher used to say, 'Everyone makes mistakes – that's why they put rubbers on the end of pencils!' We need to encourage an open culture about mistakes so that we really can learn from them.
>
> *Young person*

When we began this study, virtually nothing was known about near misses in children's services. Through it, we have shown that not only do they occur, but that they occur often. While we acknowledge that we have focused on active failures – mistakes that happen at the frontline – at the expense of latent failures embedded within the system, we have turned the spotlight on the types of near misses that can occur, how they can be averted and laid the foundations for a more detailed future study. This study would need to consider latent as well as active failures, looking beyond surface error to identify the underlying causes of incidents and patterns of error in order to devise solutions.

Indeed, this study has shown that practitioners and service users alike are key sources of knowledge about error and would welcome involvement in discussions about why things do or almost go wrong. Yet, at an organisational level, there is a dearth of mechanisms that would make it possible to learn from near misses before harm is caused to children and to prevent their reoccurrence. Our research confirmed that the current culture of blame that presides in children's services acts as a strong disincentive to such organisational learning. Evidence from the field of health – that learning from 'free mistakes' such as these can play a vital role in risk management systems, resulting in better-quality services – suggests that children involved with social services could also benefit from such an approach.

As a first step towards broadening the focus of risk management strategies in children's services from one concentrating on 'serious cases' alone, in this report we have introduced the new language of 'safeguarding incidents'. A safeguarding incident describes any unintended or unexpected incident that could have or did lead to harm for social care service users and carers. They are graded in terms of seriousness, ranging from 'no harm' incidents to serious injury and child death. This shift in focus promotes the possibility of learning from incidents before harm is caused to service users and carers. We have suggested that arriving at definitions that incorporate the risk of both immediate and long-term harm to children requires extensive consultation and debate.

The next step requires a pilot study of how best to introduce critical incident reporting within children's services. This would look at the best ways to tackle the blame culture as prerequisite to the development of such an approach. A pilot study would trial ease of reporting, develop methods for analysis and identify ways of feeding results into organisational development. Importantly, it would also look at providing time for reflection on safeguarding incidents.

We suggest that the pilot could be supplemented by a survey of how organisations charged with safeguarding children have created a culture of learning. This will involve looking at how well frontline workers are supported in their efforts to avoid error, or how they create safety, and what steps have been taken to include service users and carers in the development and evaluation of such strategies. It will focus on strategies that are in place to promote openness, time for discussion, critical reflection, building relationships and participation of service users in decision-making.

In this study, it has been shown that near misses often arise during the referral and assessment stage. Another suggestion, which we introduce here, is the development of a professional network for referral and assessment workers, based on the model of the SCIE parental mental health and child welfare network. This would help develop good practice, including promoting learning from near misses.

We suggest that collecting and analysing data on all safeguarding incidents, alongside focusing solely on serious cases, would be useful. By this means, weaknesses in safeguarding systems, particularly across agencies, could be identified. Such an approach could also seek solutions to 'no harm' incidents that are common regionally. Local Safeguarding Children Boards (LSCBs) might provide the means to develop these systems.

The findings presented in this report demonstrate that few practitioners or service users had problems identifying near misses and, given a safe environment in which they did not have to fear reprisals, were more than willing to identify and reflect on their own experiences of them.

We stress the benefits that would result from involving service users and carers in investigations about why things do or almost go wrong. This study has shown that these groups are a key source of unique knowledge about safeguarding incidents, to which practitioners, by the nature of their work, do not have access. Service users and carers demonstrate a common generosity, showing their interest in playing their part to improve services for everyone, over and above any desire for retribution for mistakes suffered personally. It has also shown that their involvement is key to the reparation that is so crucial after things have gone wrong and harm to children and/or their families has resulted.

> So most disasters are caused by the result of a sequence of smaller events, rather than a big disaster, and I think the same probably applies in social work. A disaster happens because of several smaller steps built on top of one another. These steps could be because the social worker, with the best intentions in the world, does not go and interview the mother, let's say, or the aunt, or does not go and visit the school because they just don't have time. Or they just make a judgement that 'we probably don't need that piece of information' and so a connection isn't made. And then they do not do another thing which takes them in a different direction. It's a sequence of events that leads to disaster.
>
> *Parent, individual interview*

Collecting and analysing data on safeguarding incidents, would require thought about how best to capture such learning. The development of the National Reporting and Learning System (NRLS) based at the National Patient Safety Agency (NPSA) means that health professionals are being actively encouraged to report incidents to improve patient safety. Reporting to the NRLS will mean that organisations and staff can access a range of guidance and help from the NPSA, which includes assistance in deciding how to manage incidents, how to investigate and analyse them and, crucially, how to develop a blame-free approach. We suggest exploring the development and implementation of a similar system in children's services.

Local authorities would also require increased capacity to support the expansion of risk management strategies that include the review of all safeguarding incidents. This could be in the form of a new post or responsibility shared across a number of posts, such as among childcare coordinators. The new responsibilities would involve liaising with other agencies, ensuring participation of service users and carers where they have been affected by safeguarding incidents and working with staff to identify causes of incidents. The key to the success of such an approach is its central principle of focusing on *why* incidents occurred, exploring underlying error patterns and situating incidents within a wider system – not simply stopping once professional fault has been identified. This approach is about standing back, thinking about contributory factors, facilitating participation from those with expert knowledge of safeguarding incidents – staff and service users – and trying to *understand* why things do or almost go wrong.

Given that tackling the blame culture is central to the development of such an approach, there is a need for national leadership. Here, there are opportunities to learn from the NPSA, who are working on ways to promote an open and fair culture where politicians, policy-makers and senior management as well as frontline staff understand their role in decision-making and preventing error, including reporting adverse incidents so that learning can take place. Adopting this approach in social care would allow for the coordination of the efforts of local authorities in England and Wales to report and, more importantly, to learn from mistakes and problems that could harm service users and carers. This would also enable solutions to be developed of a national as well as regional relevance to common safeguarding incidents.

> It's a very interesting way to approach it, isn't it? I'm used to taking this kind of approach from a health and safety perspective – 'Oh look, someone's tripped over the mat, it's a near miss, we need to make sure we do something about that' – but I'm not used to using that as a way of focusing on children's safety. I think it's quite a useful thing to do, and perhaps we need to build it in a bit better to the way that we think about it.
>
> *Voluntary sector worker*

This report shows that a focus on near misses may prevent serious injuries to or the deaths of children by identifying and redressing weaknesses in services intended to safeguard them from harm. It may also help prevent defensive decision-making by exploring cases where risks have been over-estimated at the expense of the child and their family. Moreover, the study itself indicated a readiness on the part of frontline staff and service users and carers to move away from a culture of blame – and the kind of risk averse practice it supports – to an open culture in which there is support both individually and organisationally for learning from mistakes. The recommendations above could help turn the feasibility of such a change into a reality, building on best practice and improving the quality of services and the safety of children.

References

1.   Department of Health (2003) *The Victoria Climbié Inquiry: Report of the inquiry by Lord Laming*, London: The Stationery Office.

2.   Barach, P. and Small, S.-D. (2000) 'Reporting and preventing medical mishaps: Lessons from non-medical near miss reporting systems', *British Medical Journal*, vol 320, no 7237, pp 759-763.

3.   Cleaver, H., Wattam, C. and Cawson, P. (1998) *Assessing risk in child protection*, London: NSPCC.

4.   Munro, E. (2005) 'A systems approach to investigating child abuse deaths', *British Journal of Social Work*, vol 25, pp 531-546.

5.   Mills, C. and Vine, P. (1990) 'Critical incident reporting: An approach to reviewing the investigation and management of child abuse', *British Journal of Social Work*, vol 20, pp 215-220.

6.   Stanley, N. and Manthorpe, J. (2004) *The Age of the Inquiry: Learning and blaming in health and social care*, London: Routledge.

7.   Johnson, S. and Petrie, S. (2004) 'Child protection and risk management: The death of Victoria Climbié', *Journal of Social Policy*, vol 33, no 2, pp 179-202.

8.   Munro, E. (2005) 'Improving practice: Child protection as a systems problem', *Children and Youth Services Review*, vol 27, pp 375-391.

9.   Rzepnicki, T. and Johnson, P. (2005) 'Examining decision errors in child protection: A new application of root cause analysis', *Children and Youth Services Review*, vol 27, pp 393-407.

10.   Department of Health (2000) *An organisation with a memory: Report of an expert group on learning from adverse events in the NHS*, London: Department of Health.

11.   Donaldson, L. (2002) 'An organisation with a memory', *Clinical Medicine*, vol 2, no 5, pp 452-457.

12.   Department for Education and Employment, Department of Health and Office, H. (2003) *Keeping children safe: The government's response to the Victoria Climbié inquiry report and the joint inspectors' report 'Safeguarding children,'* London: Cabinet Office.

13.   Taylor, A. (2004) 'New local teams to disseminate lessons learned from child deaths', *Community Care* (available at http://www.communitycare.co.uk/articles/article.asp?liarticleid=46768&liSectionID=3&liParentID=,accessed 21 October 2004).

14.   Bunting, L. and Reid, C. (2005) 'Reviewing child deaths: Learning from the American experience', *Child Abuse Review*, vol 14, no 2, pp 82-96.

15. Reason, J. (1990) *Human error*, New York: Cambridge University Press.

16. Reason, J. (1997) *Managing the risks of organisational accidents*, Aldershot: Ashgate.

17. Reason, J. (2000) 'Human error: Models and management', *British Medical Journal*, vol 320, no 7237, pp 768-770.

18. Reason, J. T. (1995) 'Understanding adverse events: Human factors', in C. A. Vincent (ed) *Clinical risk management*, London: BMJ Publications, pp 31-54.

19. Munro, E. (2005) 'Comments on draft paper 'Managing risk and minimising mistakes in services to children and families''', recipient L. Bostock, 8 April 2005 (personal communication).

20. Hetherington, R., Baistow, K., Katz, I., Mesie, J. and Trowell, J. (2001) *The children of parents with mental illness: Learning from inter-country comparisons,* Chichester: Wiley.

21. Reder, P. and Duncan, S. (2004) 'Making the most of the Victoria Climbié inquiry report', *Child Abuse Review*, vol 13.

22. Reder, P. and Duncan, S. (2004) 'From Colwell to Climbié: Inquiring into fatal child abuse', in N. Stanley and J. Manthorpe (eds) *The age of the inquiry: Learning and blaming in health and social care*, London: Routledge.

23. Stanley, N. and Manthorpe, J. (2004) 'Introduction: The inquiry as Janus', in N. Stanley and J. Manthorpe (eds) *The age of the inquiry: Learning and blaming in health and social care*, London: Routledge, p 10.

24. Munro, E. (2002) *Effective child protection*, London: Sage.

25. Munro, E. (1999) 'Protecting children in an anxious society', *Health, Risk and Society*, vol 1, no 1, pp 117-127.

26. Learner, E. and Rosen, G. (2002) *Duty first: Developing practice with children and families duty teams*, London: NISW.

27. Munro, E. (1996) 'Avoidable and unavoidable mistakes in child protection work', *British Journal of Social Work*, (1996), vol 26, pp 793-808.

28. Commission for Social Services Inspectorate (2004) 'Performance ratings for social services in England', (available at http://www.csci.org.uk/council_performance/star_ratings/star_ratings_final.pdf, accessed 19 November 2004).

29. Spencer, M. (2004) 'Why BME workers may not have agreed to be interviewed', recipient L. Bostock, 3 October 2004 (personal communication).

30. Seale, A. (2004) 'In our trust', *Professional Social Work*, March, p 9.

31. Levin, E. (2004) 'Involving service users and carers in social work education', Resource Guide 2, London: Social Care Institute for Excellence.

32. Department of Health, Home Office and Department for Education and Employment (1999) *Working together to safeguard children: A guide to inter-agency working to safeguard and promote the welfare of children*, London: The Stationery Office.

33. Silverman, D. (1993) *Interpreting qualitative data: Methods for analysing talk, text and interaction*, London: Sage.

34. National Patient Safety Agency (2004) *Seven steps to patient safety: The full reference guide*, London: NPSA.

35. Amoore, J. (2003) 'Learning from adverse incidents involving medical services', *Nursing Standard*, vol 17, no 29, pp 41-46.

36. Amoore, J. and Ingram, P. (2002) 'Learning from adverse incidents involving medical devices: Quality improvement report', *British Medical Journal*, vol 325, no 7358, pp 272-275.

37. Luckas, M. and Walkinshaw, S. (2001) 'Risk management on labour ward', *Hospital Medicine*, vol 62, no 12, pp 751-756.

38. Royal College of Radiologists (1995) *Risk management in clinical radiology*, London: RCR.

39. Cro, S. and Robotham, M. (2001) 'Learn from your mistakes', *Nursing Times*, vol 97, no 4, pp 24-25.

40. Cooper, A. (2004) 'Error theory in risk assessment', Paper given at annual conference, Royal Statistical Society, London, 7 April.

41. The Stationery Office (1989) 'The Children Act 1989', (available at http://www.hmso.gov.uk/acts/acts1989/Ukpga_19890041_en_1.htm, accessed on 29 August 2005).

42. Department of Health (1995) *Child protection: Messages from research*, London: The Stationery Office.

43. Davaney, J. (2003) 'Relating outcomes to objectives in child protection', *Child and Family Social Work*, vol 9, no 1, pp 27-38.

44. Platt, D. (2001) 'Refocusing children's services: Evaluation of an initial assessment process', *Child and Family Social Work*, pp 139-148.

45. Department of Health, Department for Education and Employment and Home Office (2000) *Framework for the assessment of children in need and their families*, London: The Stationery Office.

46. Stalker, K. (2003) 'Managing risk and uncertainty in social work: A literature review', *Journal of Social Work*, vol 3, no 2, pp 211-233.

47. Calder, M. C. (2003) *Risk and child protection*, CareKnowledge Briefing no. 9 (available at http://www.careknowledge.com/ck/application_store/portal/index.cfm, accessed 29 August 2005).

48. Calder, M. C. (2002) 'A framework for conducting risk assessment', *Child Care in Practice*, vol 8, no 1, pp 7-18.

49. Ward, H., Holmes, L., Moyers, S., Munro, E. and Poursanidou, D. (2004) 'Safeguarding children: A scoping study of research in three areas', Loughborough: Loughborough University.

50. Parsloe, P. (1999) *Risk assessment in social care and social work*, London/New York: Jessica Kingsley Publishers.

51. Parton, N. (1998) 'Risk, advanced liberalism and child welfare: The need to rediscover uncertainty and ambiguity', *British Journal of Social Work*, vol 28, no 1, pp 5-27.

52. Parton, N. (forthcoming) *Safeguarding childhood; Early intervention and surveillance in a late modern society*, London: Palgrave Macmillan.

53. Parton, N., Thorpe, D. and Wattam, C. (1997) *Child protection: Risk and the moral order*, Basingstoke: Macmillan.

54. English, D. J. and Graham, J. C. (2000) 'An examination of relationships between children's protective services, social worker assessment of risk and independent LONGSCAN measures of risk constructs', *Children and Youth Services Review*, vol 22, nos 11-12, pp 897-933.

55. Jones, D. (forthcoming) 'Making plans: Assessment, intervention and evaluating outcomes', *The developing world of the child*: Department for Education and Skills.

56. Fuller, T. L., Wells, S. J. and Cotton, E. E. (2001) 'Predictors of maltreatment recurrence at two milestones in the life of a case', *Children and Youth Services Review*, vol 23, no 1, pp 49-78.

57. Ballou, M., Barry, J., Billingham, K., Boorstein, B. W., Butler, C., Gershberg, R. *et al* (2001) 'Psychological model for judicial decision making in emergency or temporary child placement', *American Journal of Orthopsychiatry*, vol 71, no 4, pp 416-425.

58. DePanfilis, D. and Zuravin, S. J. (2001) 'Assessing risk to determine the need for services', *Children and Youth Services Review*, vol 23, no 1, pp 3-20.

59. Hollinshead, D. and Fluke, J. (2000) 'What works in safety and risk assessment for child protective services', in M. P. Kluger and G. Alexander (eds) *What works in child welfare*, Washington DC: Child Welfare League of America, Inc., pp 67-74.

60. Munro, E. (1999) 'Protecting children in an anxious society', *Health, Risk and Society*, vol 1, no 1, pp 117-127.

61. Calder, M. C. (2003) *Risk and child protection*, CareKnowledge Briefing no. 9 (available at http://www.careknowledge.com/ck/application_store/portal/index.cfm, accessed 29 August 2005).

62. Jones, D. (forthcoming) 'Making plans: Assessment, intervention and evaluating outcomes', *The developing world of the child*: Department for Education and Skills.

63. Hansen, K. (2003) 'Children at risk: How evidence from British cohort data can inform the debate on prevention: A report to the Children and Young People's Unit, DfES', London: Institute of Education.

64. Harding, T. and Beresford, P. (1996) *The standards we expect: What service users and carers want from social workers*, London: National Institute for Social Work.

65. Bell, M. (1999) 'Working in partnership in child protection: The conflicts', *British Journal of Social Work*, vol 29, no 3, pp 437-455.

66. Ashton, V. (1999) 'Worker judgements of seriousness about and reporting of suspected child maltreatment', *Child Abuse and Neglect*, vol 23, no 6, pp 539-548.

67. Ashton, V. (2001) 'The relationship between attitudes towards corporal punishment and the perception and reporting of child maltreatment', *Child Abuse and Neglect*, vol 25, no 3, pp 389-400.

68. Benbenishty, R., Osmo, R. and Gold, N. (2003) 'Rationales provided for risk assessments and for recommended interventions in child protection: A comparison between Canadian and Israeli professionals', *British Journal of Social Work*, vol 33, no 2, pp 137-155.

69. Woods, D. and Cook, R. (2002) 'Nine steps to move forward from error', *Cognition, Technology and Work*, vol 4, pp 137-144.

70. Woods, D. and Cook, R. (2002) 'Nine steps to move forward from error', *Cognition, Technology and Work*, vol 4, pp 137-144.

71. Pithouse, A. (2005) 'Comments on draft paper 'Managing risk and minimising mistakes in services to children and families''', recipient L. Bostock, 15 March 2005 (personal communication).

72. Clarke, A. (2001) *Learning organisations: What are they and how to become one*, Leicester: National Organisation for Adult Learning.

73. Fowler, A. (1997) *Gurus for government: Lessons from management gurus for local government managers*, Hemel Hempstead: ICSA Publishing.

74. Pedler, M. and Aspinwall, K. (1998) *A concise guide to the learning organisation*, London: Lemos & Crane.

75. Gould, N. (2000) 'Becoming a learning organisation: A social work example', *Social Work Education*, vol 19, no 6.

76. Isles, V. and Sutherland, K. (2001) *Managing change in the NHS*, London: NHS Service Delivery and Organisation Research and Development.

77. Fowler, A. (1997) *Gurus for government: Lessons from management gurus for local government managers*, Hemel Hempstead: ICSA Publishing.

78. Social Care Institute for Excellence (2005) 'Learning organisations: A self-assessment resource pack', London: SCIE.

79. Fook, J. (forthcoming) 'Reflective practice and critical reflection', in J. Lishman (ed) *Handbook of theory for practice teachers: A new updated edition*, London: Jessica Kingsley Publishers.

80. Fook, J. (2004) 'Transformative possibilities of critical reflection', in L. Davis and P. Leonard (eds) *Scepticism/emancipation: Social work in a corporate era*, Aldershot: Ashgate.

81. Crowley, A. (2005) 'Comments on draft paper 'Managing risk and minimising mistakes in services to children and families', recipient L. Bostock, 30 April 2005 (personal communication).

Appendix A: Systematic search strategy

Phase 1: Search strategy

Members of the project team wrote up a search strategy with input from the Knowledge Management team at SCIE (Figure 1 presents results).

Literature was identified for the scoping review from a number of sources:

- electronic databases
- handsearching electronic journals
- personal libraries of the project team.

The focus of the search reflected the twin aims of the project:

1. Explore the factors that help social work practitioners analyse risk and make safe decisions in the context of uncertainty, with a specific focus on 'close calls' and 'near misses' and the mechanisms that are in the place to promote learning from mistakes.
2. Examine the relevance to the social care sector of approaches to safety management and the reporting and analysis of 'adverse incidents', including 'near misses', developed in the healthcare sector.

The search strategy was based on preliminary discussions with researchers in the child welfare field who suggested a series of books and papers exploring reflective decision-making, conceptualisations of risk and understandings of uncertainty in everyday practice and learning from mistakes. These books and papers also covered healthcare, providing a fruitful avenue of knowledge about how allied professions, such as triage nurses, approach risk assessment. Reviewing these books, papers and policy documents generated a series of search terms, including:

- 'risk assessment' or 'risk management'
- 'decision-making' combined with 'uncertainty'

and

- 'social work' or 'health' or 'allied health professional' or 'engineering'.

In addition, documents were reviewed from the National Patient Safety Agency (NPSA) that generated health-specific terms such as 'adverse incidents'. These documents also revealed the importance of reviewing records that examine the way in which the engineering field (specifically transport and the nuclear fuels industry) approach the analysis of accidents and promote learning from mistakes.

Electronic database search

The Knowledge Management team at SCIE undertook the main literature search. A series of bibliographic databases covering social work, social sciences and the health literature were searched. To keep the size of the search manageable, the scope was limited to the previous five years (1998-2004). One database – the Cochrane Library – cannot be limited by date and so some earlier material was retrieved.

The results from each search were entered into an electronic reference library (Endnote) and 13 duplicate records removed.

The following databases were searched from 27 January to 05 February 2004. Again, to keep the search to a manageable level, the Knowledge Management team operated the following rule of thumb: only searches that produced 200 records or fewer were saved. If hundreds or thousands of records were retrieved, the search was refined in a way that cut down the output.

Table 1: Databases searched

ASSIA: Applied Social Sciences Index and Abstracts Caredata
Cochrane Library
HMIC: Health Management Information Consortium
LexisNexis Professional
MEDLINE
PsycINFO: American Psychological Association
Social Services Abstracts
Social Work Abstracts
Due to technical difficulties, ChildData was not available for searching.

Handsearching

The project team also identified the following electronic journals to be searched. These were chosen on the basis of title and likely relevance to the project aims. All journals were searched during the period noted above.

Table 2: Journals searched

Title	Years searched online, volume, issue
British Journal of General Practice	1999-2004 49(438)-54(499)
British Journal of Social Work	1998-2004 28(1)-34(1)
British Medical Journal	1998-2004 316/1(7124) –328(7435)
Children and Society	1998-2004 12(1)-18(1)
Health, Risk and Society	2000-2004 2(1)-5(3)
Journal of Family Practice	1998-2004 46(1)-53(2)

The *British Journal of General Practice* had two online volumes for 1998, and catalogue numbers had to be matched with the British Library catalogue of issue numbers.

Project team's personal libraries

In addition to the records identified from the electronic search, texts and journal papers were also identified from the authors' personal libraries. The number of additional papers and texts retrieved through this method is reported in the section below.

Phase 2: Preliminary coding and inclusion criteria

On reading the abstract, records had to be based on an empirical study or theoretical paper (excluding editorials) and meet at least one of the following criteria to be included in the scoping review:

A. concerned with approaches to risk assessment by social care practitioners or healthcare workers – specifically accident and emergency or primary care
B. examine the impact of uncertainty on decision-making by social care practitioners or healthcare workers – specifically accident and emergency or primary care
C. focus on recording, reporting and/or analysis of serious cases within social care, 'adverse incidents' in healthcare, or accidents within the engineering sector, as defined above
D. explore organisational and individual learning from mistakes and mishaps, drawing on examples from social care and health and from engineering where relevant.

Defining the inclusion criteria was an intellectually challenging and anxiety-provoking task. It involved repeatedly sharing and resharing our understanding of the project aims. Two different members of the team were working on the two main aspects of the project: one was leading on how social work practitioners analyse risk and make safe decisions in the context of uncertainty; while the other was looking at how the healthcare section approaches reporting, analysing and learning from adverse incidents. This led to both members questioning whether they were clear about the specific focus of the respective aspects of the project – for example, 'Am I looking at risk analysis and not close calls when working with social work practitioners?' And equally, 'Am I looking at risk analysis by healthcare workers rather than analysis of close calls?' This fed into a debate about what implications this had for the project and hence what records we wanted to include in the scoping review.

For example, one discussion centred on whether the concept of 'adverse incidents' or 'patient safety incidents' identified in the healthcare literature is transferable to social care settings and, if so, what kinds of incidents should we examine. Much of the literature relates to the adverse effects of discreet incidents such as accidentally administering the wrong dosage of a drug. Given the complexity of interventions in social care, such a narrow focus was likely to be of limited use in terms of the project. However, the mechanisms including the cultures that need to be in place to promote learning from such incidents appeared to be of direct relevance.

These discussions provided the opportunity, albeit draining, for teaching and learning to take place about what each member was doing, how we were approaching it and how these distinct but intertwined activities related to meeting the over-arching aim of project: to discover which learning systems need to be place to protect and promote the welfare of children and their families.

Results

The results of the various searches can be found in Figure 1.

Electronic databases

A total of 2,051 records were retrieved. Table 2a shows the breakdown by database. Duplicates arising from the initial search were removed. We do not have records about where duplicates occurred. In addition, there was duplication between literature identified within the author's libraries and the electronic search. Duplicates were removed from the electronic search records. We do not have information on numbers of duplicates identified.

A total of 678 out of 2,051 records were coded as of primary relevance to the review. This high number of references reflects the diverse aims of the study. The review aimed to underpin understanding of risk management and learning from mistakes in practice and hence had a broad interest in the literature. In this sense, it differs from a review that has a narrowly defined question, such as examining the effectiveness of a specific intervention or how best to teach a particular subject area.

Project team's personal libraries

An additional 47 papers, books and reports from the authors' personal libraries were identified as relevant to the review. While some of these were published outside the timeframe used to limit the search, they were considered important material that contextualised the literature. Of these 49, 48 were included in the literature once full papers were read and appraised.

Handsearching

This strategy led to the retrieval of 13 papers, of which three were included in the literature once full papers were read and appraised.

Results of all searches

The results of all searches identified 727 records.

Excluded records

To manage the task of reading the 678 records identified from the database search, a second phase of filtering was introduced. On reading the abstracts, a series of themes in the literature were identified, which related to the inclusion criteria. Themes that appeared beyond the scope of the current review were excluded. Among these was literature that looked at: the assessment of aggressive behaviour by psychiatric patients towards practitioners; the uncertainty faced by service users (specifically, patients asked to decide particular courses of treatment); and the general theory about how we learn, which included papers on how older people recover skills lost after strokes. Table 3 shows the themes identified in the literature by inclusion/exclusion decisions.

Table 3: Themes in the literature

Included	Excluded
Risk assessment/management by practitioners	Risk assessment/management by practitioners in field of older people
General theory of assessment	Assessment of risk to practitioners
Decision-making when uncertain as practitioner	Decision-making when uncertain as service user
General theories about decision-making	General theories about uncertainty
Specific reports of adverse incidents	General recording, not specific cases
General theory of reporting/analysis of incidents	Analysis of incidents involving technical equipment
Learning from specific incidents	General learning theory
References to National Patient Safety Agency	Learning from environmental disasters/ large-scale incidents
Governance guidance on learning from incidents/serious cases in social care	
Governance guidance on risk assessment, risk management and decision-making	

At the end of Stage 2, 388 of the 678 records were identified as directly relevant to the review.

Phase 3: Papers excluded on retrieval

The papers excluded at the initial abstract reading stage and subsequent full reading stage differed according to the inclusion criteria used.

In view of the volume of papers (196) identified within inclusion category A (risk assessment and risk management), a decision was taken at this stage to exclude non-childcare-focused papers. It had been hoped that the project team could review papers from the field of mental health, for example, but time pressures reduced our ability to look at literature outside the childcare field.

In addition, 100 papers drawn from *Community Care* magazine were excluded on the basis of descriptive rather than analytical content. Although these articles presented case studies by social work practitioners about their approaches to risk assessment and included an independent commentary on each case, no attempt was made to locate these cases within wider debates on risk assessment, nor were any generalisations made based on the cases. This seam of literature indicates that this is a popular area where practitioners both need and seek help.

On reading the abstracts examining the impact of uncertainty on decision-making, the papers excluded fell into the following categories: either the focus was too general (probability theory or gaming theory of decision-making) or too specific, such as clinical decision-making within hospital settings (decisions faced by clinicians when working with pre-term babies).

In all, 233 records were excluded on retrieval. Of these, 128 were initially categorised as A; 38 as B; 22 as C; and 46 as D (*see* Figure 1). One record that should not have been retrieved (categorised as X) was retrieved and subsequently excluded.

At the end of this stage, 155 papers were included.

Data recording and quality appraisal

Time factors meant that no papers were reviewed for quality.

The final result

A total of 206 records were included in the search.

Figure 1: Breakdown of records identified from search strategy

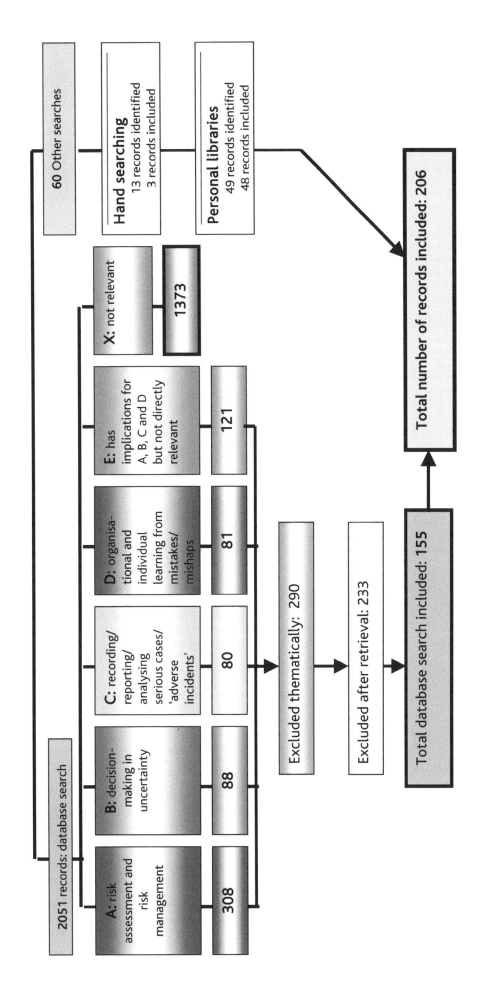

Appendix B: Topic guide

This topic guide was designed to guide our interviews and observations. It is based on knowledge from the literature and builds on our experience in the previous research sites. It aims to guide fieldwork over a sustained period.

Start-up questions

For the tape, can you tell me your name and how long you have been a social worker?

1.   Why did you choose to work here? How long have you worked here?

Primary task (why do you think you are here?)

2.   How do you see your role within the organisation?

3.   What do you think are the roles of others in the organisation?

Risk, need, thresholds and decision-making

4.   What do you understand by 'risk'? (Tease out the distinction between protecting children from immediate harm and promoting their long-term welfare, look for understanding of need.)

5.   Do you think that your own values impact on decisions about risk?

6.   What about your own background? (gender/ethnic group)

7.   Does the organisation have explicit criteria or thresholds for action? (e.g. are thresholds written down?)

8.   Can you think of a case where it's been really difficult to make a decision, where you haven't known to what extent a child was at risk/in need of protection?

9.   What helps you in your decision-making? (Follow up roles of colleagues, line management, resources – both external and internal if missed.)

10.   How do information systems help you in your decision-making?

11.   In one of the other areas, a social worker said that, while they understood that information systems were in place to protect them, they would like to take more risks in their practice. What do you think they meant by that and is that how you feel?

12.   How do you feel about the place of children and their families in the assessment process? (The literature tells us that how families experience their initial contact with social services will define the rest of their experience.)

13. Do you think that it is easy for children and families to know why decisions have been made?

14. The role of initial assessment is set up with the rest of the social work processes. It's about defining the problem – 'This is what I think the issues are' – and those initial thoughts are then passed on to the family support teams. Is that how it works here? How well does that work? (Tease out the division between risk assessment and risk management, the likelihood of cases being re-referred to the referral and assessment team once passed on to another team and the reasons for this.)

15. One of the things that comes out of research is that social workers in this country feel that the greatest risk in their job is getting it wrong, whereas social workers on the Continent feel that the greatest risk is not establishing a trusting relationship with the client. Do you think that that is a risk? (Ilan Katz work.)

16. In other sectors, risk management systems are designed with the worker in mind. To what extent do you think that social work systems are designed around the frontline social workers who do the job everyday?

Learning from close calls and near misses

17. Can you think of an example from your own practice or that of others that you would describe as a near miss? A near miss is an incident that could have gone wrong but was prevented, or did go wrong but no harm was caused. (People will often talk about the practice of others: giving practice examples may prompt discussion.)

18. What do you think caused the near miss? What were the ingredients that made it a 'near miss'? (For example, the assessment/decisions, a lucky strike in finding out something and changing the decisions.)

19. What helped prevent it from becoming a serious incident? (For example, searching for missing files)

20. Are there times when you have been involved in things, or you have seen things in your role, whereby you've been able to retrieve a situation?

21. What did you learn from it? What did others learn from it?

22. Are there any organisational mechanisms in place to promote organisational learning from near misses?

23. What about learning from good practice? Are there any organisational mechanisms in place to promote learning when things go right

Supplementary questions

NB: If not covered above, the following issues are important:

24. What happens in supervision? (Is it a supportive place for reflecting on practice or is it about line management, about meeting targets/performance indictors?)

25. Do you think that relationships with colleagues impact on decision-making? (Do they specifically help when you are feeling uncertain?)

End questions

26. Is there anything that you would like to add?

27. What do you feel about this kind of approach? (Focus on organisational learning from mistakes to provide a safer service for children and families.)

28. How do you feel about taking part?

Appendix C: Contacting participants

An email was sent to the Children and Families Committee of the Association of Directors of Social Services (ADSS) outlining the project, asking if there was interest in this approach and requesting help. Six replies were received that indicated an interest and included discussions about their current approaches to this work, references to further material and, in one case, a document outlining how the Health and Safety Executive (HSE) analysis of errors could be applied to social work.

The two local authorities chosen from the six positive responses received from the ADSS were selected for two main reasons. First, the two sites had contrasting ethnic profiles: one authority was metropolitan and the other rural. Second, and equally importantly, the project team had strong connections with the areas chosen, having worked, respectively, in practice and as a support to practice in research and social work education. One team was in the South East and the second in the North West of England.

From this initial contact in October 2004, it took a further six months to start work in the respective social work teams. This reflects the time needed to negotiate and renegotiate access through different layers of the organisation before meeting the teams to ask their permission to work with them on the project. It also meant that, on meeting the two teams, it was discovered that they were organised differently: one team had 20 members, subdivided into smaller teams each with a team leader, covering half the population of the local authority; the second team covered a smaller geographical area and had only six members including the team leader. Fieldwork was conducted over four months, from May to August 2004.

A third referral and assessment team was recruited following a request in July 2004 from the Welsh Assembly, who are in the process of conducting the Safeguarding Vulnerable Children Review. Given an initial deadline of December 2004, contacts within the Assembly helped identify and fast-track access to a referral and assessment team in South Wales. The team chosen had 20 members, supervised by a team manager and a deputy team manager. At the request of the Assembly, allied professionals were also interviewed in this location. Fieldwork was conducted from October to December 2004.

Appendix D: Error management and promoting patient safety – lessons from healthcare

1 Introduction

This is a background paper about error management and promoting patient safety within the healthcare sector. It describes the thinking behind the development of the National Patient Safety Agency (NPSA) and outlines approaches to error identification, analysis and learning. It emphasises the importance of no-blame cultures in improving patient safety.

2 Policy context

High-profile incidents such as the unnecessary deaths and harm caused to infants undergoing heart surgery at the Bristol Royal Infirmary between 1984 and 1995[1] increased pressure on the National Health Service (NHS) to improve patient safety. The report *An organisation with a memory*,[2] published by the Department of Health (DH) in 2000, turned the spotlight on the scale and nature of errors in the NHS, a tendency to seek out one or two frontline staff to blame when things went wrong and a limited capacity for learning from adverse incidents. This report was followed rapidly by an implementation strategy – *Building a safer NHS for patients*[3] – in 2001.

The policy drive following *An organisation with a memory* led to the setting up of the National Patient Safety Agency (NPSA) in July 2001 to coordinate national efforts to report and to learn from mistakes and problems that affect patient safety. At this time, research on patient safety and learning from errors in healthcare was relatively limited in the UK. A rich knowledge base on the subject was, however, found in such sectors as industry and aviation. The NHS largely drew on the experience of these sectors in developing its own safety management systems.[2]

3 Safety management and the airline industry

Following a series of air crashes in the 1970s and 1980s, the US aviation industry turned its attention to finding new ways to promote learning from errors.[4] Research found that 73 per cent of incidents were due to human factors in aircraft design and management. The term 'human factors' refers to the interaction between humans and the technology they work with.[5,6] Factors such as the layout of displays and controls in cockpits and the working culture in aviation were not providing the optimum conditions for crews to work effectively as teams.[4] The airline industry consequently implemented a safety management strategy to learn from these errors and address the root causes of the problems, which resulted in a major drop in the quantity of incidents.

The airline industry has attempted to reduce risk by encouraging staff to report errors, adverse events and near misses. The approach is based on both a carrot (staff are granted immunity when reporting) and a stick (staff face disciplinary action for not reporting). Between 1994 and 1999, one airline noted an association between reporting and risk reduction because all near misses were acted on promptly and lessons learned.[7]

Non-punitive reporting of air accidents is an essential element of our safety improvement programmes. *Pierre Jeanniot, Director General, IATA, 1998*[7]

At first sight, the focus of aviation (flying people safely from one destination to another) and that of healthcare (safe treatment of patients to improve health and well-being) appear very different. Research suggests, however, that pilots and doctors have interpersonal problem areas in common, ones that can lead to failures of communication, compliance, proficiency and decision-making.[8] The success of aviation in addressing some of these key problem areas means that healthcare may benefit from learning from safety improvements in the airline industry.

The feeling is that, in healthcare, we are not good at learning from disaster and then putting things in place to avoid it, and that other industries are much better at that than we are. And that there is a lot to learn from them, like aviation and their reporting system and the success that the industry has had in becoming much safer over a 20- to 30-year period, which is linked to reporting.

Director, National Patient Safety Agency

4 Scale of the problem

It is estimated that 900,000 patients – or over 10 per cent of patients admitted to NHS hospitals – experience an adverse incident each year. However, these figures seriously underestimate the problem throughout the healthcare system.[9] For example, there are no incident reporting systems that accurately record incidents in primary care,[9] yet this is the largest sector within healthcare and the point at which most patients first come into contact with the service. In addition, until recently, there was no clear definition of what constitutes a 'mistake' in healthcare, making it difficult to collect accurate data.[10] This is further complicated by the lack of data about normal expectations of adverse outcomes due to the natural complications of healthcare practice.[10]

5 Definitions

Until the advent of the NPSA, there was no consistent term for describing adverse events and near misses within healthcare. The literature contained a range of terms, including 'mistakes', 'errors', 'adverse events' and 'sentinel events', which are used in various combinations and sometimes without clear distinction. The NPSA developed the term 'patient safety incident' (PSI) to encompass all adverse events or potentially adverse events in healthcare. A PSI is defined as any unintended or unexpected incident that could have or did lead to harm for one or more patients receiving NHS-funded care.[11] This definition includes incidents that were prevented or that occurred but no harm was caused, respectively defined as 'prevented' or 'no harm' PSIs. Prevented PSIs are often referred to as near misses or close calls.[11-13]

The degree of harm caused by an incident is of central concern in risk management, which aims to eliminate or minimise the harmful effects of incidents.[14-16] Harm may be defined as injury, suffering, disability or death,[11] and PSIs are graded according to the degree of harm they cause (*see* Table 1). The concept of risk is strongly associated with the potential for harm and is therefore commonly seen as a negative concept.[14,15,17] However, risky situations may also turn out positively.[18] By explicitly including a category for 'no harm' incidents, the NPSA enables incident records to be balanced with positive outcomes related to risk.

> The thing with near misses is that something can be a near miss one day and an adverse event the next. By our definition, a patient safety incident is something that happened that we would not want to see happen again. It covers near misses as well adverse events because it doesn't make sense to separate them when the things that cause no harm one day can be very damaging to patients the next.
>
> *Director, NPSA*

Table 1: NPSA terms and definitions for grading patient safety incidents[19]

Grade	Definition
No harm	• **Impact prevented** – Any patient safety incident that had the potential to cause harm but was prevented, resulting in no harm to people receiving NHS-funded care. • **Impact not prevented** – Any patient safety incident that ran to completion but no harm occurred to people receiving NHS-funded care.
Low	Any patient safety incident that required extra observation or minor treatment[1] and caused minimal harm to one or more persons receiving NHS-funded care.
Moderate	Any patient safety incident that resulted in a moderate increase in treatment[2] and which caused significant but not permanent harm to one or more persons receiving NHS-funded care.
Severe	Any patient safety incident that appears to have resulted in permanent harm[3] to one or more persons receiving NHS-funded care.
Death	Any patient safety incident that directly resulted in the death[4] of one or more persons receiving NHS-funded care.

6 Error theory

Understanding the cause of adverse incidents is crucial to future prevention. Error theory is a body of work that seeks to understand the cause of error. There are two broad theories about the cause of error: the person-centred approach and the systems approach[20].

---

[1] 'Minor treatment' is defined as first aid, additional therapy or additional medication. It does not include any extra stay in hospital or any extra times as an outpatient, or continued treatment over and above the treatment already planned. Nor does it include a return to surgery or readmission.

[2] 'Moderate increase in treatment' is defined as a return to surgery, an unplanned readmission, a prolonged episode of care, extra time in hospital or as an outpatient, cancelling of treatment or transfer to another area such as intensive care as a result of the incident.

[3] 'Permanent harm' directly related to the incident and not related to the natural course of the patient's illness or underlying condition is defined as a permanent lessening of bodily functions – sensory, motor, physiological or intellectual – including removal of the wrong limb or organ, or brain damage.

[4] The death must relate to the incident rather than to the natural course of the patient's illness or underlying condition.

6.1 Person-centred approach

The person-centred approach focuses on errors made by individuals, such as pilots, nurses, doctors and anaesthetists. It views errors as the consequence of unfavourable mental processes such as forgetfulness, inattention, carelessness and negligence, and holds individuals responsible and accountable for their actions. Efforts to reduce and manage error based on this approach aim to curb such behaviour by 'naming, blaming and shaming' individuals and threatening disciplinary procedures.[20]

6.2 Systems approach

By comparison, the systems approach recognises that humans are inherently fallible and that errors will occur, even in the best organisations. It suggests that, while we may not be able to change the human condition, we can change the conditions under which people work. Consequently, focus is directed at underlying problems embedded within the system that create error-inducing conditions.[20]

6.3 Reason's Swiss cheese model

James Reason's Swiss cheese model is widely used to analyse the cause of error, including within healthcare. It illustrates how contributory factors align to cause errors. Slices of cheese full of holes represent an organisation's protective barriers. However, unlike the holey cheese, these barriers are dynamic and are constantly opening, closing and shifting their location.

Holes arise for two reasons: (i) 'active failures', which are unsafe actions committed by people in direct contact with a patient; and (ii) 'latent failures' where faults lie hidden in a system as a consequence of fallible decisions, made at managerial levels, on organisational design and processes. Latent failures may include lack of training, inadequate supervision, absence of procedures and faulty or poorly designed equipment. An error occurs when holes in the protective barriers align.[13,14,20-22]

This model locates the dynamics of individual actions within the context of a systems approach. The aviation industry adapted Reason's model to suit their purposes (*see* Figure 1). More recently, Charles Vincent *et al*[14] have also adapted it to identify the factors that impact on the safety of mental health patients, including patient-based, task-based, individual, environmental, organisational, managerial and institutional factors.

7 Approaches to learning from errors

The aviation industry, when examining its methods for dealing with error, found that 'naming, blaming and shaming' individuals consistently failed to reduce the occurrence of errors. Instead it generated a secretive and defensive culture. Once the industry adopted a systems perspective, drawing attention away from individual blame and focusing instead on systemic issues, a more effective way to reduce the occurrence and minimise the effect of incidents emerged.[4]

Figure 1: Aviation-based illustration of Reason's Swiss cheese model of human error causation[23]

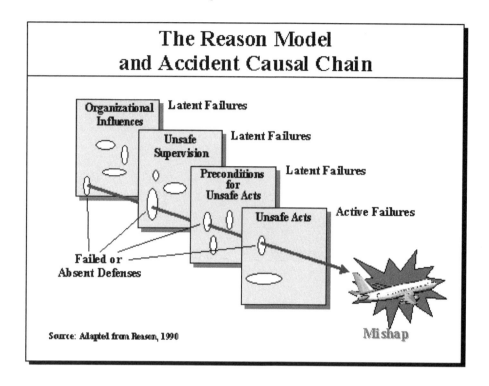

The medical profession is in the process of changing from a person-centred to a systems approach to error management. Currently there are various methods of assessing past practice with the aim of improving patient care. These include:

- confidential inquiries following PSIs
- a national reporting system for PSIs that involve medical devices[2]
- morbidity and mortality conferences held as part of medical training programmes to discuss medical errors[24]
- grand rounds that are seminar-like exchanges between academics and service professionals for discussing good practice
- peer reviews that subject individuals' work to review by others who have equivalent or superior knowledge.

These forums operate by examining individual cases and, with the benefit of hindsight, reconsidering the clinical decision-making processes undertaken by physicians. However, while informative, they have not prevented PSIs. This is because they focus on individual practice at the expense of understanding the context within which individual practice takes place. This suggests that an individual's knowledge and skills are the key determinants of patient outcomes.[25] Yet research shows that errors are usually due to multiple contributory factors, and they tend to have recurrent patterns, with similar circumstances leading to similar incidents regardless of the individuals involved.[9,20,21]

Such forums rarely consider or tackle the root causes of error. In 2003, an American survey of 114 house officers on training programmes revealed that the hospital atmosphere inhibited talking about errors in 27 per cent of cases, and in 48 per cent of conferences, key issues such as being overworked were not addressed.[26] This suggests that current methods for assessing past practice are missed opportunities for learning from errors.[24]

A key strategy in aviation's approach to improving safety has been the introduction of a universal incident-reporting system for identifying and addressing the root causes of incidents and implementing changes based on findings from analysis of the reports. A main feature of this reporting system is emphasis on the value of reporting near misses as well as actual errors.

Near misses occur much more frequently than incidents that lead to harm. As far back as the 1940s, H.W. Heinrich demonstrated that, for each industrial incident causing serious injury, a far greater number of incidents result in minor injuries or no injury at all: at a ratio of 1:29:300[21] (see Figure 2).

Reporting near misses significantly increases data available for analysis. Although near-miss incidents do not result in harm, they are, nonetheless, potentially harmful. Therefore, reporting them may also highlight organisational deficiencies and help identify what prevents incidents from leading to harm, enabling preventive strategies to be put in place before serious incidents occur.[12-14]

8 Establishing reporting systems

Establishing an effective reporting system is dependent on the features outlined below.

8.1 Safety culture

The development of an open and fair, blame-free culture in which individuals feel able to report and discuss adverse incidents is fundamental to an effective reporting system.[21,22,28] This is likely to take many years. The evolution of critical-incident reporting systems in non-medical domains has taken several decades.[29]

Figure 2: The Heinrich ratio[27]

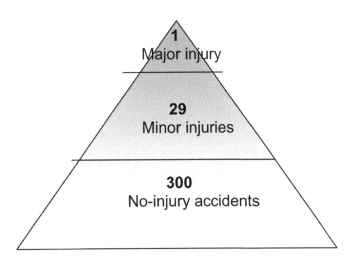

8.2 Reporting near misses as well as serious incidents

As with aviation, emphasis on reporting near misses as well as serious errors is key to establishing an incident-reporting system. Including incidents with positive outcomes may help quell apprehension about reporting – individuals are less likely to feel guilt and shame in reporting incidents with good outcomes, and others are less likely to apportion blame.[13-15,30]

8.3 Ethics

Surveys of patients confirm that most want to be informed if an error has been made,[31] and in many countries, medical practitioners are ethically obliged to disclose errors. For reporting systems to be ethical and gain support, they need an open, honest and accurate process for dealing with the individuals and/or families concerned, and issues of data confidentiality must be addressed.[32]

> We are suggesting with our 'being open' policy that patients must be involved if they've been harmed, no matter what level of harm. So a patient might be approached and told that: 'This nearly happened to you, but it didn't quite. But because we want to learn for the future, and we want to make healthcare safer, we want to involve you in the investigation. Is that OK?' So we try not to undermine their confidence, and by involving them, hopefully they will have more confidence in us because they'll see us really wanting to learn from things.
>
> *Director, NPSA*

8.4 Patient reporting systems

The NPSA is committed to ensuring that the experiences of patients inform its work and priorities. Patients or their relatives are encouraged to report experiences of NHS care that have resulted in harm or put them at undue risk. (For more information, please visit www.npsa.nhs.uk/ppr.) To encourage people to report mistakes, the NPSA does not keep people's names on record. All information about the mistake is held anonymously. This means that the NPSA does not investigate individual cases, but rather uses the information to try to stop the same mistakes happening again.

9 Reporting incidents

Encouraging staff to report all errors and adverse events is a challenge. Staff must be fully aware of the system in place and confident that it will be effective at improving practice safety without being a threat to those doing the reporting.[14] Common disincentives to reporting include lack of time and the perception of extra work for already overburdened staff, fear of disciplinary action, mistrust in the system, scepticism due to previous experience of ineffective reporting systems, uncertainty of what actually constitutes an error, and belief that only serious errors should be reported.[12] However, other things have been shown to encourage reporting.

9.1 Keeping reporting distinct from disciplinary action

One key incentive is to ensure that a reporting system for learning from errors is clearly distinct from disciplinary and litigation bodies.[12-14,30] If criminal activities are discovered, these should be addressed in the legal manner, but individuals should not fear punishment for errors that they did not intend.[20] Where legal protection for those reporting errors has been reinforced, as in Australia and New Zealand, incident reporting systems have gained acceptance and credibility.[12] (*See* the Australian Patient Safety Foundation [APSF] website – www.apsf.net.au – for more information.)

9.2 Confidentiality

Another key incentive for incident reporting is the guarantee of confidentiality. There is some debate about whether confidentiality or anonymity is the best approach. While full anonymity may appear more appealing from the perspective of the person reporting the incident, this may hinder follow-up of a report and in-depth analysis.

The APSF removes identifying information from the data it collects. This anonymous data is then keyed into an aggregated database that allows all health units to receive comparative information linking their performance with other 'like' organisations. The de-identified data allows aggregation of low-frequency events at an international level and is therefore very effective for identifying and coordinating system-based strategies to better detect, manage and prevent problems.

9.3 Promoting the value of reporting

Promoting the value of reporting to staff is crucial. This ethic could be embedded in professional schools and graduate training programmes.[17] Ingraining the importance of reporting for staff also demands rapid, meaningful and ongoing feedback on the benefits made in practice as a consequence of reporting.[12,14,22,30]

9.4 Simple and short reporting forms

Forms that are simple and quick to complete encourage reporting.[12] Following the launch of their easy-to-use reporting system, Central Manchester and Manchester Children's University Hospital NHS Trust saw an increase of 53 per cent in the number of reported incidents from January to July 2003. In line with recommendations from the NPSA, their forms cover:

- the date of making the report
- the name of the reporting organisation
- reporter details (name, job title, telephone, email)
- apparent outcome of incident in terms of harm
- when the incident occurred (date/time)
- where the incident occurred (speciality/location)
- who was involved (patient and staff descriptions)
- what happened
- what immediate action was taken.[33]

10 Analysis

Identifying and reporting incidents is only part of the process. It is equally important to find out why they happened and what can be done to prevent or minimise the likelihood of them happening again.[11,13] The 2001 Department of Health report *Doing less harm*[34] suggests a three-stage process by which local NHS organisations should analyse the information gathered in incident reports:

1. grading the incident
2. assessing its risk to patients
3. analysing its root causes.

10.1 Grading incidents

As already noted, incidents should be graded according to the severity of harm actually caused: no harm, low, moderate, severe, death. Incidents should then be graded according to their most likely consequences should they happen again. Thus near-miss incidents can be judged according to their potential severity. This grade is plotted against the likelihood of the incident's recurrence, as shown by the incident-grading matrix in Table 3. This matrix can be used to indicate the potential future risk of an incident's recurrence to patients and to the organisation.

10.2 Analysing root causes

Not all incidents need to be investigated to the same extent. The incident-grading matrix is intended to help identify PSIs in need of immediate in-depth analysis – i.e. category red incidents – and those that would be more suitable for less intensive, aggregated analysis with other similar incidents.

Table 3: Incident-grading matrix[34]

Likelihood of recurrence	Most likely consequences*				
	No harm	Low	Moderate	Severe	Death
Almost certain					
Likely					
Possible					
Unlikely					
Rare					

POTENTIAL FUTURE RISK TO PATIENTS AND TO THE ORGANISATION

RISK: ▮ Very low ▯ Low ▮ Moderate ▮ High

---

⁵ In *Doing less harm*, the terms used are: none, minor, moderate, major, catastrophic. They have been changed here to match the NPSA definitions, which came after publication of *Doing less harm*.

The suggested technique for analysing incidents is root cause analysis (RCA). This is a structured investigation that works backwards from an incident to identify the root causes of the problem and the actions necessary to eliminate it.[3, 35, 11] It should involve a relevant range of professionals and should consider all perspectives on the incident, including those of patients and their families.[30] The whole process should be documented on a computerised database, recording the incident, results of investigations and any subsequent recommendations.[14]

The NPSA's RCA toolkit (www.npsa.nhs.uk/health/resources/root_cause_analysis/conditions) suggests various tools for analysing an incident, as shown in Table 4. Incidents should be investigated promptly, while they are fresh in people's minds.[14, 17]

Table 4: RCA tools

Brainstorming unstructured	A group puts their ideas forward in a structured or manner. These are written down and prioritised. A facilitator is essential.
Brain writing	Similar to brainstorming, except that it allows individuals to generate ideas anonymously and in a short time-frame. At the end of a set period (approximately 10–15 minutes), a facilitator collects the written ideas, organises them and prioritises them.
Fishbone diagram	The head of the fishbone represents a specific issue; the spines show the factors to be considered. This may be used to analyse a specific issue or problem, not the whole incident.
Five why technique	This essentially means developing a questioning attitude and never accepting the first reason given.
Barrier analysis	This is a review of all the barriers (controls) that were in place, and which should have stopped the incident occurring or mitigated its impact. Each barrier is identified. Did it succeed? If not, why not? If it failed, was it a causal or influencing factor?

11 Conclusions: Seven steps to patient safety

Building patient safety requires changes in many areas, including a change in culture in the NHS. Evidence from other industries shows that, if the culture of an organisation is safety conscious and people are encouraged to speak up about mistakes, then safety is improved.[3] In summary, the NPSA has identified seven key steps to patient safety, outlined in Table 5.

Table 5: The seven steps to patient safety[36]

Step 1	**Build a safety culture** Create a culture that is open and fair.
Step 2	**Lead and support your staff** Establish a clear and strong focus on patient safety throughout your organisation.
Step 3	**Integrate your risk management activity** Develop systems and processes to manage your risks and identify and assess things that could go wrong.
Step 4	**Promote reporting** Ensure your staff can easily report incidents locally and nationally.
Step 5	**Involve and communicate with patients and the public** Develop ways to communicate openly with patients and listen to them.
Step 6	**Learn and share safety lessons** Encourage staff to use root cause analysis to learn how and why incidents happen.
Step 7	**Implement solutions to prevent harm** Embed lessons through changes to practice, processes or systems.

These steps provide a simple checklist to help plan activity and measure performance in patient safety. They also help healthcare organisations meet clinical governance, risk management and controls assurance targets. They provide a clear framework for improving the safety of NHS patients.

References

1. Department of Health (2002) *Learning from Bristol: The Department of Health's response to the report of the public inquiry into children's heart surgery at the Bristol Royal Infirmary 1984-1995*, London: The Stationery Office.

2. Department of Health (2000) *An organisation with a memory: Report of an expert group on learning from adverse events in the NHS*, London: DH.

3. Department of Health (2001) *Doing less harm: Improving the safety and quality of care through reporting, analysing and learning from adverse incidents involving NHS patients: key requirements for health care providers*, London: DH.

4. Westwood, R. (2004) 'Team resources management and human factors', paper given at 'Mental health 2004' conference, Church House, 5-6 May.

5. Human factors research and technology division, Ames Research Center (available at http://human-factors.arc.nasa.gov, accessed on 29 August 2005).

6. Federal Aviation Administration (no date) 'FAA Human Factors Workbench' (available at http://www.hf.faa.gov/Portal/ShowProduct .aspx?ToolType=True&ProductID=147', accessed 12 August 2005).

7. Fyle, J., Gregor-McGlynn, A. and Jokinen, M. (2002) 'Flying lessons: risk management and the NPSA', *RCM Midwives Journal*, vol 5, no 10, pp 322-323.

8. Helmreich, R.-L. (2000) 'On error management: lessons from aviation [Editorial]', *British Medical Journal*, vol 320, no 7237, pp 781-785.

9. Department of Health (2000) *An organisation with a memory: Report of an expert group on learning from adverse events in the NHS*, London: Department of Health

10. Alden, C. (2001) 'Doctors and mistakes – part 1: incident inevitability: the domino effect: so why do doctors make mistakes?', *Hospital Doctor*, 22 March, pp 32, 34-35.

11. National Patient Safety Agency (2004) *Seven steps to patient safety: The full reference guide*, London: NPSA.

12. Barach, P. and Small, S.-D. (2000) 'Reporting and preventing medical mishaps: Lessons from non-medical near miss reporting systems', *British Medical Journal*, vol 320, no 7237, pp 759-763.

13. Amoore, J. (2003) 'Learning from adverse incidents involving medical services', *Nursing Standard*, vol 17, no 29, pp 41-46.

14. Luckas, M. and Walkinshaw, S. (2001) 'Risk management on labour ward', *Hospital Medicine*, vol 62, no 12, pp 751-756.

15. Royal College of Radiologists (1995) *Risk management in clinical radiology*, London: RCR.

16. Amoore, J. and Ingram, P. (2002) 'Learning from adverse incidents involving medical devices: Quality improvement report', *British Medical Journal*, vol 325, no 7358, pp 272-275.

17. Cro, S. and Robotham, M. (2001) 'Learn from your mistakes', *Nursing Times*, vol 97, no 4, pp 24-25.

18. Cooper, A. (2004) 'Error theory in risk assessment', paper given at conference, Royal Statistical Society, 7 April.

19. National Patient Safety Agency (2004) *Seven steps to patient safety: The full reference guide*, London: NPSA..

20. Reason, J. (2000) 'Human error: Models and management', *British Medical Journal*, vol 320, no 7237, pp 768-770.

21. Donaldson, L. (2002) 'An organisation with a memory', *Clinical Medicine*, vol 2, no 5, pp 452-457.

22. Dean, B. (2002) 'Learning from prescribing errors', *Quality and Safety in Health Care*, vol 11, no 3, pp 258-260.

23. Luxhøj, J.T. and Kauffeld K. (2003) 'Evaluating the effect of technology insertion into the national airspace system', *The Rutgers Scholar* (Rutgers, The State University of New Jersey) (available at http://rutgersscholar.rutgers.edu/volume05/luxhoj-kauffeld/luxhoj-kauffeld.htm, accessed on 12 August 2005).

24. Pierluissi, E., Fischer, M., Campbell, A. and Landefeld, C. (2003) 'Discussion of medical errors in morbidity and mortality conferences', *Journal of the American Medical Association*, vol 290, no 21, pp 2838-2842.

25. Wachter, R.M., Shojania, K.G., Saint, S., Markowitz, A.J. and Smith, M. (2002) 'Learning from our mistakes: Quality grand rounds, a new case-based series on medical errors and patient safety', *Annals of Internal Medicine* (Philadelphia), vol 136, no 11, pp 850-852.

26. Wu, A.W. (2003) 'Do house officers learn from their mistakes?' *Quality and Safety in Health Care*, vol 12, no 3, pp 221-228.

27. Department of Health (2000) *An organisation with a memory: Report of an expert group on learning from adverse events in the NHS*, London: DH.

28. Ioannidis, J.P.A. and Lau, J. (2001) 'Evidence on interventions to reduce medical errors: An overview and recommendations for future research', *Journal of General Internal Medicine*, vol 16, no 5, pp 325-334.

29. Barach, P. and Small, S.-D. (2000) 'How the NHS can improve safety and learning by learning free lessons from near misses [Editorial]', *British Medical Journal*, vol 320, no 7251, pp 1683-1684.

30. Heget, J.-R. (2002) 'System innovation: Veterans' Health Administration National Center for Patient Safety', *Joint Commission Journal on Quality Improvement*, vol 28, no 12, pp 660-665.

31. Singer, P.A., Wu, A.W., Fazel, S. and McMillan, J. (2001) 'An ethical dilemma: Medical errors and medical culture – An error of omission/Commentary: Learning to love mistakes/Commentary: Doctors are obliged to be honest with their patients/ Commentary: A climate of secrecy undermines public trust', *British Medical Journal*, vol 322, no 7296, pp 1236-1240.

32. Monagle, P., Robb, B., Driscoll, S. and Bowes, G. (2002) 'Organ retention following paediatric and perinatal autopsy: Where to from here?' *Journal of Paediatrics and Child Health*, vol 38, no 4, pp 405-408.

33. Department of Health (2001) *Doing less harm: Improving the safety and quality of care through reporting, analysing and learning from adverse incidents involving NHS patients: key requirements for health care providers*, London: DH.

34. Department of Health (2001) *Doing less harm: Improving the safety and quality of care through reporting, analysing and learning from adverse incidents involving NHS patients: key requirements for health care providers*, London: DH.

35. Lewis, R. (2003) 'Don't slip up: How PCOs are road testing patient safety', *Primary Care Report*, vol 5, no 8, pp 16-19.

36. National Patient Safety Agency (2004) *Seven steps to patient safety: The full reference guide*, London: NPSA.